ADVANCE PRAISE

"*Independent Study That Works* is a must-read for anyone teaching or advising high school students. Geraldine Woods's experience creating, implementing, and refining an independent study program for hundreds of students and their mentors translates into an informative guide for those wanting to introduce, expand, or improve independent study opportunities. Her book provides a framework for mentors that enables student ownership while providing guidance, flexibility, and the chance for students to teach peers what they've learned."

 —Thomas M. Kelly, Ph.D., Head of School, Horace Mann School

"*Independent Study That Works* outlines an approachable way for homeschoolers to implement an independent study course for their middle and high school students. Homeschoolers can use this book to guide them as they launch independent studies with a small family, multi-family co-op, or even a solo student. The book's warm style invites you to become part of an educational adventure. You can do this, and your students will benefit."

—Jennifer Kaufeld, author of *Homeschooling For Dummies, 2nd Edition*

"Geraldine Woods's *Independent Study That Works* achieves exactly what it sets out to do: it celebrates a student-centered approach to learning that honors the individual talents and interests of each student. She deftly makes the case for creating an independent study and provides all the direction you might need. She has condensed decades of experience into an accessible and beneficial package."

 —Bob Matthews, English Teacher and Director of Independent Study, Episcopal High School, Bellaire, TX

"Even decades later, I still think about my experience in Ms. Woods's Independent Study class. It was an extraordinary invitation to a lifetime of creative exploration. I love that this wonderful book will help extend that invitation to so many more students for generations to come."

 —Jordan Roth, president of Jujamcyn Theaters

T0366785

INDEPENDENT STUDY THAT WORKS

DESIGNING A SUCCESSFUL PROGRAM

NORTON BOOKS IN EDUCATION

INDEPENDENT STUDY THAT WORKS

DESIGNING A SUCCESSFUL PROGRAM

Geraldine Woods

W. W. NORTON & COMPANY
Independent Publishers Since 1923
New York • London

This work is intended as a general information resource for educators. It is not a substitute for appropriate professional education or training or clinical supervision. Any URLs displayed in this book link or refer to websites that existed as of press time. The publisher is not responsible for, and should not be deemed to endorse or recommend, any website, app, or other content not created by it. The author, also, is not responsible for any third-party material.

Chapter 1 photo © Farng-Yang Foo
Chapter 2 photo © Alexis Stein
Chapter 3 photo © Rosy Aurora
Chapter 5 photo © David Berenson
Chapter 6 photo © Samuel Schuur
Chapter 7 photo © Dorin Azerad
Chapter 8 photo © Jordyn Cosme

For information about permission to reproduce selections from this book, write to Permissions, W. W. Norton & Company, Inc., 500 Fifth Avenue, New York, NY 10110

For information about special discounts for bulk purchases, please contact W. W. Norton Special Sales at specialsales@wwnorton.com or 800-233-4830

Manufacturing by Versa Press
Production manager: Katelyn MacKenzie

Library of Congress Cataloging-in-Publication Data
Names: Woods, Geraldine, author.
Title: Independent study that works : designing a successful program / Geraldine Woods.
Description: First edition. | New York : W. W. Norton & Company, 2022. | Series: Norton books in education | Includes bibliographical references and index.
Identifiers: LCCN 2021036088 | ISBN 9781324019664 (paperback) | ISBN 9781324019671 (epub)
Subjects: LCSH: Independent study--Handbooks, manuals, etc. | Education, Secondary.

Classification: LCC LB1049 .W6267 2022 | DDC 371.39/43--dc23

LC record available at https://lccn.loc.gov/2021036088

W. W. Norton & Company, Inc., 500 Fifth Avenue, New York, N.Y. 10110
www.wwnorton.com

W. W. Norton & Company Ltd., 15 Carlisle Street, London W1D 3BS

1 2 3 4 5 6 7 8 9 0

For my students,
whose delight in learning ignites my own.

Contents

Acknowledgments   *ix*

Introduction: Education as It Was Meant to Be   *1*

1 The Independent Study Program   *9*

2 The Project   *27*

3 The Seminar   *47*

4 Adaptations   *59*

5 Subject Area Tips   *77*

6 Independent Study as a Homeschooling Option   *99*

7 Independent Study Units Within a Traditional Class   *109*

8 Beyond the Classroom   *123*

Appendix A: Using Common Core Standards
to Evaluate Projects   *135*

Appendix B: Sample Forms   *139*

Index   *145*

Acknowledgments

While I was working on this book, I spoke with dozens of students and teachers from many states and three different continents. No matter how busy they were or how inconvenient the time zone was—in the middle of a pandemic, no less!—all were gracious and generous in sharing their experiences and ideas. They reminded me, in every interview, why I love the teaching profession. I am extremely grateful to all of them.

I am also grateful to my school, Horace Mann, which trusted me to establish and run the independent study program. I owe an extra portion of gratitude to Avram Schlesinger, the current director of independent study at Horace Mann, who provided documents, Zoom links to presentations, and all sorts of valuable information.

Finally, I thank the publishing professionals who guided me as I worked on this book: Carol Collins, the sort of editor every writer wants; Sophia Seidner, an agent who always offers an encouraging word and a brilliant suggestion; and Jamie Vincent, editorial assistant, whose timely and gentle reminders kept me on track.

Education as It Was Meant to Be

I t is a sunny afternoon in May. I am sitting on the edge of the school's athletic field with my student, Josh, an earnest senior speed-talking his way through an analysis of the novel he has just read. A few yards away, his peers loll on blankets spread over the grass. Some are officially done for the day; others are cutting class.

Although Josh and I are not in a classroom, we are both "in class"—independent study, to be precise. All year Josh has been reading the novels of science fiction author Philip K. Dick and watching films based on them, comparing Dick's alternate reality to historical events. I wasn't familiar with this author when school started in September, but I have been reading along with Josh. Our weekly meetings follow a set pattern: I begin by asking what he has done since I last saw him. I review his notes and we talk or, more accurately, Josh talks and I chime in with an idea or suggestion for further research. I end the conversation by asking what he will accomplish before our next meeting. As Josh lists a hefty amount of work, I express doubt that he'll have enough time. "Sure I will," he replies. "Seniors don't do homework in the spring." When I remind him that what he plans to do is, in fact, homework, Josh shrugs. "You didn't give me this homework," he explains. "*I* gave me this homework."

Therein lies the advantage of independent study. One of them. There are more, without doubt: a chance to satisfy curiosity and pursue an intellectual or artistic interest. The opportunity to go narrow and deep instead of wide and shallow, to adapt pedagogy to suit the student instead of the other way around. A way to refine research skills and source evaluation, to learn time management, to take responsibility for one's own education and, paradoxically, to create a community of learners.

WHY, AND WHY NOW

I wrote *Independent Study That Works: Designing a Successful Program* because I believe in the value of the independent study program that I directed for a quarter century at New York City's Horace Mann School. In my view, it comes closest to the way education is meant to be, the polar opposite of the teach-to-the-test, schedule-to-suit-the-bus-company model too often imposed on educators. I stepped away from full-time teaching a few years ago, but Horace Mann's program is flourishing, as are other independent study programs that I describe in this book. Some are similar to the one I established; others appear quite different but rest upon the same values. I assume you're reading *Independent Study That Works: Designing a Successful Program* because you want to start an independent study program or make changes to one your school already has. Or perhaps you're interested in applying independent study methods to curricular units in an otherwise traditional class. Maybe you're a home-schooler searching for a new approach. *Independent Study That Works: Designing a Successful Program* will help you accomplish those goals.

Speaking of goals, if there was ever a time to reach for them, it's now. When COVID-19 struck, many teachers heroically pivoted from in-person to hybrid to online learning and back again—several times! Being forced to change has proved that change *is* possible. More than a few educators have not wanted to go back to normal as the threat of contagion recedes, because existing strategies have not worked well for too many students. The beauty of independent study is that it is not a lofty pedagogical theory. It is practical in all learning formats, for a range of age groups and skill levels, in public and private schools.

Let me backtrack a moment to tell you how I came to independent study. I was teaching a full range of English classes when I heard that my school would offer a new course, the "interdisciplinary independent study seminar," the following year. Twenty students had enrolled, each with a different project. Among them were Daniela (portrayal of scientists in film and literature), Jared (history of political cartoons), Stacey (psychology of superstition), Melissa (ancient Greek art), Greg (ethical issues in computer programming), and Andreas (biology of leeches—live ones!). The course design put all those kids in one room twice a week. Was I interested? Yes, I was. I was also terrified. What does an English teacher know about leeches or political cartoons? How could I keep twenty kids on task without common benchmarks? Most frightening to me: what would we do in seminar?

Obviously, I took the job. Over the next couple of decades, my answers to those questions evolved, but the basics of the course remained the same:

- *project:* a student-proposed, yearlong research inquiry, science experiment, or creative work
- *mentoring:* close supervision by an adult, usually but not always a faculty member
- *product:* concrete expression of learning, such as a paper, lab report, interactive website, story, artwork, or performance
- *presentation:* at least one by each student per grading period, during which the student teaches something learned through project work

That is what my independent study class looked like, but yours doesn't have to. In fact, it probably should not be an exact copy, because the independent study you implement should reflect your own goals and your students' needs. To that end, in this book I describe how other schools manage independent study effectively. I also discuss independent study in the context of homeschooling, and I explain how to adapt independent study methods to a traditional class format and to online learning.

WHO AND WHERE

Some schools designate independent study as a program for "gifted" students only. I must confess that I would rather listen to a fingernail scratching on a chalkboard than sort kids according to whether they are "gifted" or "not gifted" (for one label implies the other). Students perceive the sorting, and they often live up or down to expectations. I am not denying that people have strengths and weaknesses, but calling students "gifted" generally means that their strengths mesh with the expectations of the classes they are in. Thus an independent study program that is open to myriad types of projects suits myriad abilities. In my view, independent study should not be limited to the "best" students as defined by the usual metrics. Instead it should celebrate all participants *at* their best, as they study or create something that is meaningful and satisfying, in a way that works for them. Through the years, I have found that independent study may be the brightest moment in a struggling student's academic career. There is no need to make special accommodations for a student's learning style. The course itself is an accommodation, designed by each student to match their abilities and aspirations. The best part? Confidence gained through independent study carries over to other classes and life arenas. One success sets the stage for another.

Nor must independent study be limited to schools blessed with ample resources. Granted, I worked in a school with a healthy budget, a well-stocked library, and other material support. All that was wonderful, but none of it was crucial. I have seen great independent study programs in all sorts of settings, both well funded and underfinanced, many of which I describe in this book. At least one teacher must take charge, but volunteers from faculty and staff, as well as community members and alumni, can be mentors as well. And people do volunteer. Nearly every time I have asked someone to supervise a project, the answer has been yes—actually, more like *yes!* Nurturing kids' interest and the chance to learn something new can be powerful lures, even for the busiest teachers.

What exactly do I mean by independent study?

Type "independent study" into a search engine and hundreds of links pop up. There are teacher-designed modules for homeschoolers, as well as online, asynchronous courses. Many links take you to sites offering a complete, standardized curriculum for remote learning, supervised by a licensed teacher. Others offer a personalized learning program, with a teacher custom-tailoring a course of study to fit an individual's needs. Some links lead to experiential learning opportunities—internships and the like—in which students receive credit for an activity outside the traditional classroom.

These offerings, valuable though they may be, tend to move students along a preordained, teacher-designed path. Participants may be enthusiastic, even passionate about their work, but they have less agency and ownership than they do in the sort of independent study I discuss in *Independent Study That Works: Designing a Successful Program*. Furthermore, in most of these programs students report to an audience of one, the authority who awards credit. I prefer to center the student in every way possible: in a network of sources, adult guides, and a learning community of peers.

BEDROCK

Underlying the independent study program I developed, and for the most part, the variations I describe in *Independent Study That Works: Designing a Successful Program*, is a bedrock comprised of four elements.

Student power and responsibility

When you are a student, much of what you do is defined by THEM, the teachers or administrators who rule your day, your semester, and your academic career. And that is as it should be, mostly. I prefer a doctor whose medical school curriculum was fashioned by experts, and I imagine you do, too. Yet surely there is room earlier in the educational timeline for some autonomy. Stronger guardrails are required for middle schoolers than for college freshmen, but within limits, students should have as much power as possible. With power comes responsibility, as a multitude of superheroes have reminded us. If independent study participants fall behind or mess up, they cannot plead "we're just kids."

Adult guidance

Of course, they *are* just kids. Their reach exceeds their grasp, they get distracted, and they lack experience. That is why each student should pair with a mentor who, at frequent intervals, checks the quantity and quality of work, provides context and suggestions, and gives feedback.

Flexibility

Anyone who has done original research knows that it is a journey of discovery: what you thought was a side topic turns out to be essential or vice versa. Artistic efforts, too, bring the unexpected. The act of research or creation *requires* change because learning affects the learner. Independent students define initial and interim goals but should remain open—and able to justify—alterations.

Performance

Who doesn't love an audience? Lots of people, actually, but performance—communicating what you have learned—is nevertheless a skill worth learning. Independent study participants should have the opportunity to present a portion of their work to their peers (either classmates or networked homeschoolers) and to the wider community, preferably more than once, so they can apply the lessons learned on the first occasion to the next.

YOUR PATH

I spent a fair amount of time with you, the reader, as I wrote this book—the *you* I imagined, that is. Some days you were in a large, rule-ridden school, fighting for your students' right to be seen as individual human beings rather than as official statistics. Frequently you were quietly circulating throughout a classroom you had decorated with things you love: students' best assignments, posters celebrating your subject, a jarred bouquet of multicolored pens. From time to time I saw only your face. It was frustrated: *School should be better than this.* Or joyful: *They understand the lesson!* And always determined: *I will make a difference.*

I hope the information in this book supports your efforts, whoever and wherever you are, no matter the direction you wish to take with independent study. In reference to that last point, here is a road map. Read everything, or head directly to the chapters that support your journey. Be sure to stop along the way to read the "spotlights" in each chapter. They give you glimpses of independent study projects and the students and mentors who worked on them. Now for the specifics:

- Chapter 1 describes the program I established and directed, my reference point for everything I believe about independent study.
- Chapter 2 goes into detail about the project, the individual work each student takes on. I explain how to evaluate proposals, pair students with mentors, keep track of each student's progress, and assess the fruits of their labor.
- Chapter 3 focuses on the independent study seminar, which gathers the group at set intervals to share their knowledge. I discuss preparing students to teach what they have learned, scheduling presentations, and evaluating seminar work.
- In Chapter 4, I showcase independent study's adaptability by presenting varied programs: a four-year sequence, a single-mentor class, a middle school unit, career-oriented internships, and more.
- In Chapter 5, I turn to subject areas, offering advice specific to projects in these categories: language arts, foreign language, STEM, social studies, the arts, and interdisciplinary work.
- Chapter 6 speaks directly to homeschoolers, explaining how the principles of independent study apply in that setting. I also discuss practical matters, such as forming a collaborative seminar, submitting records to state and local officials, and documenting the independent work for college admissions officers and potential employers.
- Chapter 7 focuses on independent study within a traditional course. I describe small changes that make a big difference in teacher and student roles, assessment, and classwork. I suggest a number of assignments, all adaptable to various subject areas and grade levels, and provide an in-depth look at three classes employing independent study techniques.
- In Chapter 8, I widen my vision to what lies beyond the classroom: administration, the school as a whole, the community, and parents. Drawing on my experience with each group, I show you how to forestall or solve problems. I also travel beyond the school years, offering glimpses of the effect a successful independent study program can have on your students' future.

I will let Ted, a former student, have the last word of this introduction. Perhaps he will inspire you, as he inspired me, to give independent study my best: "Through independent study I learned that my interest was a signal worth following. The lack of explicit instruction was an empowering experience, closer to the platonic idea of what education should be."

CHAPTER 1

Farng-Yang's copy of the Foo genealogy, the basis for his
project exploring the experience of his family in the context
of Chinese history.

The Independent
Study Program

When you were a student, did you ever sit in a classroom musing about what you would do differently if you were the teacher? Maybe devote an extra two weeks to a favorite topic and delete the one you found so-o-o-o boring? The hypothetical course you came up with probably informs what you are doing now as an educator, though I doubt you possess the absolute power you once imagined your teachers had. That dreaming child of long ago would have loved independent study, which offers the opportunity not only to plan an ideal course but also to make it real. Within limits, naturally.

In this chapter I explain the structure of the independent study program I established and directed. The program evolved through the decades, and it is evolving still. But the basics have remained the same, because independent study builds on qualities we all share: curiosity, pride in our achievements, and the desire for connection with others.

The examples in this chapter are drawn from high school students, but the structure of the program is adaptable for younger grades. See Chapters 4 and 7 for more information on independent study in middle school; Chapter 6 describes independent study in a homeschool setting.

THE BASICS

Independent study at Horace Mann is a year-long, full-credit elective that allows students to pursue projects based on their academic or creative interests. It does not satisfy any subject-area requirements, and it may not be an add-on to the normal student load. (The school sets a limit of five, full-credit courses per year.) A few more facts:

- Students (mostly twelfth graders, but occasionally some younger students) apply in the spring prior to the year in which they will take the course.
- Applicants write a proposal and revise it several times, in consultation with faculty, until they have a viable project.
- Accepted students begin work on their projects during summer vacation, so they can hit the ground running when school resumes.
- All students are assigned mentors. The pairs meet once or twice in the spring to flesh out plans; throughout the following year, they meet weekly.
- Students log their work online or in a notebook. They cite sources they have consulted and submit notes or progress photos every week.
- Once per grading period, students create a tangible expression of what they have learned: a paper, an exhibit, a performance, computer code, and the like.
- Students also participate in a seminar with a cohort of fifteen to twenty students.
- The seminar meets five times per ten-day cycle. During class, students take turns teaching their peers a portion of what they have

learned. Generally, each student teaches one full-period and one half-period class per semester.

- The faculty member who leads the seminar personally mentors several projects and meets every two weeks with students mentored by others.
- Students earn grades ranging from A+ to F, based equally on their project and seminar work, assessed holistically.

Did you notice that I didn't mention a grade requirement for entry? There isn't one. To quote the course description: "The most important factor is motivation; you have to want to learn about your subject, preferably to the point of mania." (I go into detail about evaluating the suitability of students for independent study in Chapter 2.)

You may wonder about all those meetings—when and where they take place. The "when" is any mutual non-class period, including lunch. The "where" may be an office or an empty classroom, but I have held "office hours" on radiators, brick walls, and athletic fields, too. I have also visited science labs and art or music studios. One memorable project (solar power) took me to the roof, which to my great relief was flatter than it appeared from the ground. And of course with virtual learning, meetings take place online.

Because the program prizes independence, not anarchy, the students' path is edged by sturdy guardrails. The purpose of regular meetings,

creative consciousness in artificial intelligence
science of music therapy
writing a memoir, novel, poetry collection
peacemaking efforts in the Middle East
concussions and sports
the physics of Greek mythology
Einstein's theory of relativity reflected in the arts
Don Quixote
domestic violence
composing and performing an aria
green architecture
religion in Shakespeare's plays
music composition and songwriting
behavioral economics
effect of interior design on health
family farms and agribusiness
social media and mental health
writing a screenplay
reunification of Germany
oral histories of immigrants from Asia
politics and nuclear weapons in North Korea
building and programming a robot
video journalism
media bias
historical survey of weight-loss fads
Arthurian legends
biofuels
art and bipolar disorder
acting styles

logs, and tangible products is to hold students accountable for their work, not to regulate the work itself. That is where the independent part of the program resides. A sampling of independent study projects appears on the previous page.

THE PROJECT: WHAT THEY DO AND WHY THEY DO IT

During the first few years of the program, I told prospective applicants that independent study projects landed in one of two baskets: "research-based" or "creative." I stopped making that statement when it dawned on me that students were paying no attention to my categories. Good thing, too! The work they were doing was great, whether it was all research (the Chinese Cultural Revolution, the plays of Oscar Wilde, autism), all creation (composing an aria, painting portraits, writing short stories) or some of each. A sampling of independent study projects appears on the previous page.

- One student combined math and fashion—mapping two-dimensional cloth into three-dimensional garments, using calculus to determine the arc of a curve, and so forth. She designed a collection of clothing based on mathematical principles; a stand-out piece was a dress made entirely of neoprene hexagons.
- Another student surveyed the history of ceramics, gradually narrowing his focus to porcelain produced in Jingdezhen, China, a renowned center of the art. He delved into the economics, design, and politics of ceramics and then made his own pieces, inspired by the works he had studied.
- Yet another student's project combined social studies, science, and the arts. The student researched the steelpan, a percussion instrument that originated in Trinidad and Tobago. After studying the history and culture associated with the steelpan, he performed experiments to determine the effect of different metals and frequencies on the instrument's sound. Then he wrote and performed an original song.

Independent study also frees students—and teachers!—from preconceived notions of the nature of education, such as how knowledge can be acquired. Most students do their research from online or printed sources, but a good number also interview experts or participate in internships. (Anyone in this last category also has an on-campus faculty mentor and participates in seminar.) Ben, whose project was a comparison of news coverage in the media of three countries, spoke at length with a reporter from the *New York Times* to gain an insider's perspective. Andrew interned at a natural history museum, using their lab to analyze the chemical composition of meteorites. Rebecca met frequently with a sociologist as she gathered data on the effectiveness of anti-bullying programs. Some of the "experts" she consulted were middle school girls.

Ending Point: The Product

Another barrier independent study can break is how knowledge may be expressed. One long paper per grading period is a common choice, but a series of shorter papers may also be appropriate. Students have built interactive websites, where not only their mentor and classmates but also a wider audience can view their work. Many have curated art exhibits, staged plays, given concerts, produced podcasts, and made films. I have seen architectural models coded by energy consumption; hand-carved, custom-wired electric guitars; illustrated guides to the nine circles of Dante's Inferno; and a hovercraft that rose a few inches off the ground while carrying a student. With some projects, the goal is to inform others: Chiara chose a wall display for her project on access to reproductive health care. After studying the economics of the issue (who has insurance, how much it costs), she looked at legal issues. On an enormous map of the United States, Chiara listed relevant state laws. The map was on display in a school hallway for a month and drew a wide audience. Because some rights and restrictions are tied to age, students were curious about what their own situation would be if they lived in another area of the country. Caroline's project was part personal, part historical. She researched her family's history in Korea and the details of her parents' immigration to the United States. She noted which elements of Korean culture they maintained in their American household: food, etiquette, celebrations, and so forth. For her final product, Caroline wrote a computer program that gradually changed her image. Her attire shifted from a *hanbok* (a traditional Korean dress) to jeans, T-shirt, and sneakers.

The bottom line: independent study prioritizes learning, not rules. What is studied, how it is studied, and how knowledge or skill is displayed—all these factors arise organically from the project. The adults do not exercise undue control, nor do they cede it. Students' inventiveness is validated, but their work is held to a high standard. (For practical advice about the application process and supervision of independent study projects, see Chapter 2.)

Starting Point: Motivation

The variety of independent study projects is as wide as students' imagination, which is to say, limitless. Sometimes a project arises through serendipity. To pass the time during a long car ride one summer, Daniel and his father listened to an audiobook, Michael Lewis's *The Big Short*. By the time they arrived at their destination, Daniel knew he wanted to learn more about behavioral economics—how and why people make financial choices. For a year or so he read books and watched TED talks on the topic and, when the opportunity presented itself, turned his interest into an independent study project. "I would have been doing the work anyway," Daniel says, "because I genuinely loved it." His project culminated in a research paper, the longest he'd ever written, explaining the principles of behavioral economics. Daniel has no complaints about the workload. "Independent study was interesting. Sometimes, if I had something important to do, like study for a really scary math test, I would procrastinate by picking up my independent study reading instead," he says.

For Annie, independent study was a way to explore a talent. "I've always had trouble writing essays and things like that," she explains, "so I wasn't looking forward to the required research paper for my junior English class." But Annie had always been interested in film, and when her English teacher suggested she report her findings in the form of a screenplay, Annie was eager to try. To her delight, she found that dialogue flowed easily. She had no trouble expressing her ideas in this format, and independent study provided a venue that played to her strengths. Her project also satisfied an emotional need. Annie wrote a script for a road-trip film during an intense phase of the pandemic; through the project she "lived vicariously because the characters got to interact with each other in ways I craved but couldn't do."

Diana's project also arose from a deep need: a desire to connect with her heritage. Diana's grandparents, who were born in Iran, often recited verses to her from the *Shahnameh*, or *Book of Kings*, an epic poem that recounts the history of Persia from ancient times through the seventh century. Diana began her project by reading the poem in translation. (Diana doesn't speak Farsi; she decoded a small portion of the original text with her grandmother's help.) She looked at images based on the *Shahnameh* that elevate the status of the shah, or king, and compared them to European art that also glorifies a figure, such as a Renaissance altarpiece. Next, Diana read *The Rubaiyat of Omar Khayyam* and examined visual art associated with it. Finally, she studied the works of contemporary Iranian writers and filmmakers, with special emphasis on art with feminist themes. In college, Diana continued her independent study and made a presentation to her art history class. "The media tends to present only a narrow, negative view of Iran. People don't see the country's rich intellectual and artistic tradition, which starts with the *Shahnameh*," she says. To share that heritage with others, she first had to explore it herself.

SPOTLIGHT:
Making History Personal

Farng-Yang belongs to the seventy-fifth generation of his family, as documented in a seven-volume genealogy stretching back more than two millennia to the Qin Dynasty of China. (The photo at the beginning of this chapter is his family's copy of the genealogy.) The official goal of Farng-Yang's independent study was to situate his family's history in the context of world events, specifically the history of China and, more specifically, the World War II years, when Japan invaded the country and his grandfather was interned in a labor camp. But there was a personal goal as well. "As a kid I was always trying to figure out where I fit in," explained Farng-Yang, "and there was no formal structure to learn this information outside of independent study." Work on the project enabled Farng-Yang to forge an even stronger bond with his father, who helped him translate some of the genealogy, and with his grandfather, who patiently recounted his life story, creating an oral history that is itself a treasure. To complete the picture, Farng-Yang also explored his mother's family history. "I'm glad that I was able to do this project. When I started, I didn't have all the skills yet, and this was a good way to learn about historical sources and primary sources." His father was also pleased with Farng-Yang's independent study: "His work has contributed to my understanding of our family history" and "reassured me that our family history will not be lost to future generations."

Ed's project was a response to a gap in the curriculum, specifically a lack of literary works by LGBTQ writers in English classes and similar omissions in history and other courses. Ed looks back at the education he received and deems it "selective learning." He explains, "Whole sections of the classics, of poetry especially, had been cut out, especially love poems. The omitted material could make a big difference by keeping gay students from feeling alone." Ed read extensively with the goal of putting together an annotated list of readings that teachers could incorporate into existing courses—works by Virginia Woolf, Claude McKay, and James Baldwin for English class; books by Martin Duberman and other historians for social studies; and classical selections from Cicero and Julius Caesar for Latin class. Ed read literary criticism, too, and asked knowledgeable alumni to suggest titles. Ed reflects, "I didn't know what was going to happen when I talked about this topic, but for the most part people reacted very positively. Just to see that people actually cared about what I was saying was very powerful." Ed's project raised awareness and resulted in additions or substitutions to the list of required reading.

For Sophie, independent study was a chance to dive into a subject she was "passionate about but hadn't had the opportunity to explore": children in crisis. She'd done volunteer work but until this course had not found a way for this topic to "live in an academic environment." Sophie first researched refugees fleeing war in West Africa and then read about children conscripted as soldiers. She studied gender violence and recovery from trauma. Her independent study, she believes, was an "inflection point" that led directly to her college major in political science with a focus on international development and human rights. She also notes the influence of independent study on her career choices: a stint with Teach For America and her current position as chief of staff at a charter school network serving under-resourced communities.

STUDENT AS TEACHER: THE SEMINAR

When independent study landed on my schedule many years ago, I was pleased but also flummoxed. The person who'd designed the course and shepherded it through the approval process had moved to another school. Thus it was up to me to decide what to do with twenty seniors pursuing wildly divergent projects in the same room twice a week. I considered assigning general readings on the philosophy of knowledge or perhaps selecting one pivotal year and having students examine its art, politics, and scientific discoveries. I rejected these approaches because I didn't want to cut into the time available for students' individual projects. I also vetoed a plan to simply let the kids work while I roamed around offering helpful hints. The room was small, and in those pre-internet days, research outside of a library was not easy. Plus, some projects involved composing music and doing science experiments. Stashing the musician with his piano in one corner and the biologist with her plants in another was not an option.

I decided that if students could be in charge of their own learning, they could be in charge of the seminar, too. The most obvious configuration was a short statement from each student: "This is what I learned last week and what I'm planning to do next week." But what would a quick skate across the surface of each project accomplish? Finally I hit upon this idea: students would take turns running the class, once per grading period. I called it a "presentation," but I didn't want it to be a summary. Instead, students would teach a portion of what they had learned to their peers.

A word to homeschoolers: seminar is for you, too. If you teach more than one child, each can do an age-appropriate independent project and share the results. You can also organize a seminar within your homeschooling network, as I explain in Chapter 6. Teachers of younger children will find information in Chapters 4 and 7 on creating a seminar-like atmosphere in their classrooms.

SPOTLIGHT:
"I'm Going to Drop the Course"

There are nervous presenters and there are *nervous* presenters. Nina was in the latter group. Two months into the year and ten minutes before her first presentation to the independent study seminar, she showed up on my doorstep and said, "I'm going to drop the course." Her voice was shaking, and I thought she was joking. We had gone over her lesson; she was studying photographer Robert Frank and was planning to show slides from *America*, his groundbreaking work. She knew the material perfectly! But Nina did not laugh. "I can't do this. I'm sorry to disappoint you, but I can't go in there and talk to all those people."

"It is not 'all those people,'" countered her supportive friend, Shefali. "It is just our class. You *can* do it." I of course agreed, but friends in this situation are more powerful than teachers, so I let Shefali take the lead. "Look at me," she said. "Show the slides and explain them to me." And that is exactly what Nina did. "It helped that their attention was on the photos and that the room was dark," she said recently when we talked about her experience. "I still don't like giving presentations at work and outsource them to a colleague if I can." One thing that helped her: "They asked nice questions. They weren't trying to outsmart me the way people did in some classes." Her verdict: "It's a privilege to study what you are interested in and to hear about other people's passions." And no, she did not drop the course.

The Power of Continuity

One morning some years ago, Pete was on stage with his band, playing what I am sure was very good music. I couldn't appreciate it, though, because I was too busy glaring at him. Two hours earlier, I'd marked him absent. He had cut my class! "No," Pete corrected me when we spoke recently. "I cut *our* class. I cut Ariane's presentation." It says a lot about the power of the bonds forged in seminar that more than two decades later, Pete still feels bad about skipping out on a classmate's presentation in order to practice with his band.

You don't build the sort of loyalty Pete felt toward Ariane and his other classmates in a single day. That's a disadvantage of independent study programs that conclude with one presentation, a culminating moment when students proudly display their work. The venue is often an assembly in which students talk about their projects or a sort of learning fair with booths displaying the work. (Both types often went virtual during the pandemic.) In some schools, students present their independent study projects to a jury of faculty and experts, who review what the student has accomplished, ask questions or make comments, and evaluate the work. These are great events, without doubt; public recognition of students' labor is always valuable.

That said, I prefer the ongoing seminar format because it harnesses the power of continuity. It does not preclude the crowning moment of a one-and-done presentation, when the final results of an experiment are in, the film is ready for screening, the musician performs, the artist exhibits, and the research paper or novel is printed. But sharing the process is so much better than only seeing the finished product! An example: for his final presentation, a student who'd researched World War II naval warfare staged the Battle of Midway in the school's pool. As his enthusiastic helpers steered model ships to strategic positions, he explained what was at stake and outlined each side's strategy. It was a damp, uncomfortable lesson (the class and I perched on a tiled ledge), but no one seemed to mind. We had watched the project develop over the course of a year. What did a few splashes matter? We were *invested.*

Investment, in turn, builds connection. If you witness the raw beginning, the mighty effort, the I-don't-know-yet stage, the final product lands with a surprisingly emotional punch. As Pete put it, "You felt like you were in something together and you wanted to do a good job, to support each other. It's the 'we-ness,' the cohesiveness of the group." Woody Howard, Pete's mentor, agrees. "The seminar teaches students that they have a responsibility to each other."

The interdependence of the seminar, I've come to realize, strengthens students' independence. One year the seminar was scheduled immediately following my poetry class. I often invited poets to discuss their work, and if guests lingered, I couldn't abandon them. At times, therefore, I was a couple of minutes late to seminar. The first time this happened I raced to my classroom, readying apologies—which I didn't need, because the kids had started without me. I was surprised at first, but when I thought a bit, the whole thing made sense. The real teacher of that day's class, the student presenter, was in the room, so the class could begin. I should note here that although these were wonderful kids, they were still kids. In my traditional courses I'd occasionally had to give a couple of them my teacher frown along with a stern "see me after class." Their sense of responsibility originated in the seminar, not in my or their personalities.

Having several opportunities to present also gives students interim goals. No one wants to come in without something to say, and the only way to be sure that doesn't happen is to do the work. As one student put it (in less polite language than I reproduce here), "You can blow smoke for three minutes, but not for forty." Another advantage is that, unlike a single, year-end presentation, an ongoing seminar gives students a chance to apply presentation skills they learned from the first presentation to subsequent classes. Daniel, for instance, says he learned that "it takes a really long time to write words on the board" during his first presentation, when he ran out of time before he could cover key points. For his second presentation, Daniel prepared slides and got much better results.

With multiple presentations, important skills have time to develop to the point where they're more likely to endure. Will, who studied carbon nanotubes and went on to an engineering career, noted that his independent project was his entry into actual science, a field in which "presenting the work is as important as doing the work" when it comes to applying for grants or talking with clients. Jordan, a student-playwright-turned-producer, sees the independent study seminar as "the beginning of a lifelong exploration of how to find and contribute to a community with which you share your work." Peter cites the seminar as a means of "learning to structure your ideas in a way that can be communicated to others."

Repeated opportunities to present can also be calming. Most kids are tense the first time. Getting through it, even enjoying it, builds confidence, and they approach the second round in a better frame of mind. After the third round, they are so good at explaining their work that I can send them off to other classes: one student presented her project on Spanish cinema to advanced language students; another gave a speech on concussion prevention to the physical education faculty. A dedicated young scientist hauled a tank full of leeches to an elementary school science class, where he explained the animals' unique qualities while I kept eager little hands away from his subject matter.

Presentation Examples

Woody Howard, an experienced and treasured mentor, described the average seminar session as "participating in a tossed salad" because the topics and presentation methods are so varied. The variety makes it hard to illustrate what the seminar is like. Any presentation I show you offers only a quick glimpse, akin to the descriptions of an elephant offered by blind men in the parable. Nevertheless, here are two.

NEWS COVERAGE COMPARISON

Ben's project compared news coverage in various papers during the 2006–2007 school year. His presentation outline:

Homework

Students will read the articles I distribute. Half will receive "Bush Vows to Find Common Ground with Congress" (*New York Times*, 9/15/06) and half "Bush Strongly Defends Plan on Prisoners" (*Wall Street Journal*, 9/15/06). They will answer the following questions in two or three sentences each:

1. Based on what you read, summarize the events.
2. Describe Bush's response.
3. Do you agree with the president?

I will collect their responses and see whether different papers produced different answers.

DISCUSSION

15 minutes What's the story? I will open with an attempt to pin down the facts. I will read four responses that differed, and we will try to find a middle. This will lead into a discussion about bias. What is it? Where can you look for it? How do you recognize it?

10 minutes I will speak briefly about what I analyze when I read articles on the same topic from the six selected newspapers: structural differences (what's first, what's buried in the middle), quotations (who speaks, how long, positive or negative about the topic), graphics (size, prominence), content (what's included and excluded), language (connotations, effect of word choice).

10 minutes I'll explain what I found generally true about each paper, over the course of my reading—their biases as I perceive them. Then I'll ask them to look at the homework articles again. (They all have both now.) How is the president portrayed? What should readers look out for when reading these newspapers?

The presentation included the student's spreadsheet displaying quantifiable differences in coverage by region in a random issue of the paper. He charted geographical areas and topics such as arts, politics, and business. (See Table 1.1.)

TABLE 1.1: Comparison of News Coverage

Newspaper	Top geographical areas covered (percentage of space on page 1)	Topical break-down (percentage of space on page 1	Graphics
New York Times	National (42.3%) Middle East (34.9%)	National politics (25.1) Foreign relations (18.8) Society (15.1)	Wounded soldier in Iraq Voter casting his ballot Football player getting academic help
Wall Street Journal	National (74.6%) Europe, Asia, Africa (22%) Middle East (3.4%)	Business (48.5%) Politics (26.9%)	Drawing: man painting donkey Two screenshots from animated films Graphs: ethanol, unemployment
Clarín	National (46.5%) US (30.8%) Other South America (11.4%)	Local news (37.4) Crime (30.8%) Society and pop culture (8.8%)	Crime photo
Le Monde	National (44.6%) Middle East (18.2)	Foreign relations (54.1%) Art (23.7)	Drawing: Ahmadinejad Photos: Al Jazeera worker, William Styron portrait

GREEN BUSINESSES

Devin's project focused on the development of green businesses. This presentation took place during the pandemic in a hybrid setting (some online, some in the classroom). For homework, students completed a survey at footprintcalculator.org to find out how many Earths would be necessary to sustain their current lifestyle. Devin began the presentation by discussing students' results and reactions. Next came a series of slides explaining the business of solar power in the United States and China. Here's the outline:

Slide 1: Talk about solar, China vs. the US, companies

Slide 2: Go over homework from footprintcalculator.org
- Are you shocked by the amount of energy you have used?
- What leads to the majority of your carbon emissions?
- What can you do to improve the amount of carbon you output?
  - vehicles (last presentation)
  - energy (solar, this presentation)
  - food (what I'm looking into next, plant-based meats)

Slide 3: Recap last presentation on influx of green businesses

Slide 4: Discuss solar energy as one of these fields that have benefited
- takes what's around us and uses it as energy
- sun emits enough power each second to satisfy the entire human energy demand for more than two hours
- Bell Labs invented the first useful solar cell more than 60 years ago
- types of solar panels
- last year solar obtained 1.8% of the energy marketplace vs. the 85% of fossil fuels
- 10% of renewable energy market

Slide 5: What is halting the solar industry? (efficiency, cost)

Slide 6: Show chart and explain how solar has continued to reduce prices
- more efficient deployment
- better material and composition design
- mass production
- in the US, reduction in cost will increase the solar power produced by at least 700% by 2050

Slide 7: Discuss efficiency
- in the last ten years or so that solar photovoltaics (PV) have taken off, allowing for more research

- panels nearly 30 percent efficient
- 44.5% percent efficiency in certain laboratory tests using advanced cell structures

Slide 8: US compared to China
- US leads in innovation, China far ahead in commercial sales
- 7 of the world's top 11 solar-panel manufacturers are in China
- 60% total annual solar cell manufacturing is in China
- China—$160 billion on solar expansion
- US—$250–550 billion on oil subsidies

Slides 9–11: Discuss JinkoSolar (Chinese company)

Slide 12: Discuss future of solar power

Now you've taken a "tour" through my school's independent study program, the sort I might give to prospective students. I go into more depth with those who express interest, hoping that if the course is a good fit, they will enroll. My hopes are the same for you (on the teacher and administrative level, naturally). Join me in the following chapters as I describe independent study on the day-to-day level.

CHAPTER 2

Lexi, a high school senior, wrote this book to teach
young children about healthy eating habits.

The Project

As I made my way through a crowded hallway one day, a student introduced himself and launched into an explanation of the independent study project he hoped to work on during the following year. I told him to meet me later that day and continued onward. He nodded and kept talking—and walking—right into the women's lavatory. (This was before gender-neutral facilities were available.) When he realized where he had ended up, the young man turned bright red and backed away as fast as he could. I do not remember what he wanted to study. I do remember thinking that whatever it was, I would make it work. You don't waste enthusiasm like that.

Enthusiasm, though, is not enough. There has to be a curriculum, for what is independent study but a curriculum designed for one? But not *by* one. Especially not *by one inexperienced kid* who doesn't know, for instance, that attempting nuclear fusion isn't the best first step for a budding physicist, given that the world's best scientists still haven't done it. Not to mention practical details like, you know, radioactivity. Nevertheless, students should have as much say-so as possible in designing their projects. They may not be experts in pedagogy or subject matter, but they are experts in one important thing—themselves.

Putting together an independent study project isn't the work of a moment, even for a short-term unit. For full-year or semester projects, the process may begin months before the first day of class. Or it may actually be part of the class, as it is at Urban Academy, a public high school in New York City. Students who elect to take a course called "Choose Your Own Adventure" come in with a topic, which they refine over the next couple of weeks with their teacher's help. Bottom line: it doesn't matter when this work happens so long as it does.

Nearly every successful independent study project starts with a written proposal and a conversation about that proposal. Sometimes many conversations! The goal is not to exclude students or quash their ideas; it's to help them craft a viable project. In this chapter I describe what to look for, in both the project and the student proposing it, and explain how to guide students in defining their goals and methodology. I also discuss various aspects of supervision, including finding mentors and supporting their efforts.

A GOOD PROJECT?

It's easy for me to evaluate a proposed independent study project in my field, English. I know whether a literary work or writing task will strengthen skills and challenge students to think. Show me a math or a science or a history project, however, and I draw a blank. Ditto for an artistic project. You want to compose an opera? And stage it? Sounds great, but . . .

I turn to my colleagues and sometimes to outside experts for help in evaluating proposals. (Some schools and homeschooling networks convene a panel for this task.) Many of those I consult ask me to identify the criteria for a valid project, not specific to one field but rather the educational principles underlying all. Good question! You should answer that question, too, so that it reflects your own values and those of your school. Here's what I look for, with some suggestions about how to determine the answer.

Worthwhile content

The project should merit the time and effort the student invests in it. As you weigh its value, imagine the project as a course. Given sufficient student interest and an ideal world with no time or budget restraints, should the school offer the class? Should the homeschooler teach it? Why or why not? The answer highlights the project's value and flaws.

Originality

Independent study isn't intended to copy a course already offered, no matter how appealing the idea of one-on-one meetings with a favorite teacher may be. Mentors generally volunteer their time or, if they receive a stipend, earn pennies per hour. It's simply not fair to ask a teacher to give a duplicate class as an independent study. Homeschooled students, of course, already benefit from their teacher's focused attention. What to watch out for in this setting is a project that's too similar to a previously studied unit, an appealing but unhelpful activity for a student who lacks confidence.

Skill development

Content and product aren't always the most important elements of a project; introducing or reinforcing skills also has value. Common Core Standards, while about as much fun to read as the tax code, can guide you here. (For more information and a sampling of Common Core Standards, see Appendix A.) Don't forget about nonacademic skills the project may foster, such as locating experts and building a network.

Sustainability

I'm not using this word in the environmental sense, though I applaud projects that are respectful of the earth's resources. Instead, I'm referring to the likelihood that the project will hold the student's interest, a tricky category because if people are anything, they are unpredictable. But you or someone who knows the subject can make an educated guess. For example, a college friend considering a linguistics class dropped the idea when she saw that the first month was devoted to the schwa (the sound of the *a* in *about*). A project requiring a similar level of dedication needs extra scrutiny.

Solid, but flexible

The project sets the student on a journey, so it's not unreasonable to ask about the destination. What do you want to know/create/achieve with this? What are reasonable interim goals? Solid answers to these questions are important, but there should also be room to grow. A ten-page proposal that nails down every detail is too limiting. Look for some flexibility, or accept the ten-page plan and assume it will evolve. You can even encourage it to evolve, as Houston's Episcopal School does, by asking students to write a two-page report on their progress halfway through the grading period. "That's the moment when there is a pivot," says Bob Matthews, who directs the program. "They understand that what they thought they were going to do may not be achievable, but this other thing may be."

Feasibility

Be practical: every project needs an appropriate mentor (more on that topic later in this chapter), as well as sufficient space and equipment. Is there a spot where student scientists and artists can experiment, rehearse, or make things? How about storage? Prowl around: a corner of a lab or studio, a closet, a garage, or a dead-end corridor may meet the need. What about supplies? Are they available? Affordable? The vast amount of free information on the internet reduces the book bill, but science experiments and artistic projects involve more than written material. Find out what the school owns. Homeschoolers, check your inventory. For whatever is lacking, inquire at nearby schools, homeschooling networks, and community organizations. Some may allow access to their facilities or lend equipment.

Lexi has always been interested in nutrition, the subject of her independent study. "Originally I thought I would concentrate on the science, the biological aspect of nutrition. But I got much more involved with the socioeconomic aspect," she says. Lexi's internship at a company selling organic beverages was instrumental in changing the focus of her project. Her job was to source ingredients, which she discovered were extremely expensive. "The company promotes living a nutritious life, but that is not an option for many people. You really don't have a choice if the most nutritious food is too expensive for your budget," she explains. Lexi also notes that geography plays a role. "Some people live in a 'food desert' where there are no nearby stores selling fresh fruits and vegetables. There may be no grocery stores in the neighborhood at all, only small markets or delis selling processed or junk food."

As she investigated food inequality, Lexi also evaluated what schoolchildren are offered through national lunch and breakfast programs. She read a number of studies about children's nutritional choices. "It turns out that knowledge is really important. Too many kids don't know what to eat and how food affects their health," Lexi says. "I didn't know much about nutrition either when I was a little girl. I never really understood the food pyramid the FDA [Food and Drug Administration] designed to show you how much of each food group you should eat. It was shaped like a triangle, but I ate from a round plate!" The FDA eventually changed the pyramid to a more relatable circle graph ("MyPlate"), but Lexi thought still more was needed to get the message across. So, she wrote a children's book, *Nutritious and Delicious: A Children's Guide to Living Their Happiest and Healthiest Life*. (A photo of the book introduces this chapter.) "I wanted it to be fun, to teach seven-year-olds about nutrition with activities like coloring, word jumbles, and an exercise game tied to the spelling of their names." One page is a fill-in-the-blanks story about "Tommy," who is packing his lunch for school. "I make a point of saying he chooses a dessert," Lexi remarks. "I don't want them to think that certain foods are prohibited or that good nutrition is punitive. It's all about balance." Because of pandemic restrictions, Lexi could not visit elementary schools in person to lead children through the activities, but she hopes teachers will use her book in future classes. She herself plans to continue studying nutrition and health policy. "Independent study for me was a checkpoint, a chance to see that this is really what I want to do. It is not only a health but also a justice issue when access to good nutrition is not available to everyone. Working on this will be my career," she concludes.

READY . . . WELL, ALMOST READY

Sophie had a list of questions. What physical reactions occur when a brain is concussed? Can head injuries be prevented? How should coaches deal with concussions? Her project was fully formed and ready to roll.

Others' plans weren't as detailed. Kevin knew that he wanted to write poetry and that he loved music, but that's as far as he'd gotten. Ted was, by his own description, "a tech guy" who was also interested in history and military technology. He wanted to research how advances in weaponry affected historical events. Beyond that, he wasn't sure. For these two it would be *lather, rinse, repeat* until their projects took shape. By that I mean they would have to write proposals, respond to feedback, and resubmit them . . . as many times as necessary until everyone was satisfied. Appendix B provides a sample proposal form. This is by no means the only format. Some schools have students secure signatures from parents, counselors, and current teachers. Others ask for a more detailed work plan or annotated source list. Choose whatever you like, but do ask for a written proposal, even if you're a homeschooler and hear your student talk about the project every evening during dinner. Having to formally explain the project makes the student think more deeply about the amount and type of work; putting it on paper or uploading it to a class website carries a stronger sense of commitment.

Once you have the first draft of the proposal, discuss it with the student. Here are some common first-draft problems and ways to remedy them:

- *The proposal lacks detail.* Ask clarifying questions. For Kevin: Do you set your poems to music? What sort of process works best for you when you write? What matters most, sound or meaning? For Ted: Which historical periods interest you? Would you rather focus on developments in one era or would you prefer to compare weapons from different time periods?

- *The project is beyond the student's abilities.* Students who have already taken basic courses can explore an advanced topic, but beginners will drown if they jump directly into the deep end. Help them find their level. Middle school science teacher Andrea Champagne of University Liggett School recommends mapping. In the case of the (fictional) nuclear fusion proposal I referred to earlier, she wouldn't simply say no. Instead, she and the student would map everything the student must learn before attempting the project: the nature of subatomic particles, the laws of thermodynamics, and so forth. As the paper fills with topics, the student sees that the initial proposal isn't achievable but also what *can* be accomplished—such as an experiment with chemical reactions.

- *There isn't enough time.* Writing a novel isn't the work of a semester, nor is studying genetic traits in five generations of avocado plants. Faced with a proposal with an unrealistic time frame, focus the student on process. When will you determine the plot and characters? How many pages will you write each week? Or, ask the student to change the focus. Avocado pits sprout within weeks, so analyzing germination rates under varied conditions is feasible.

Neither you nor the students have to work on the proposal alone. Teachers from other departments may have suggestions, as may parents or community members. Reaching out is itself a valuable skill! As for the students named above, both pursued terrific projects. Kevin, who decided that "some poems are meant to be read, and some are meant to be performed," published a book of poetry and wowed the audience with his poem "Smile I, Not in a While" at a school assembly. Ted investigated the boomerang and *atlatl* (spear-thrower) in Stone Age hunting, the pivotal role of the English longbow in the Battle of Agincourt, and the evolution of World War I tanks and anti-tank armaments.

MATCHING THE RIGHT STUDENT WITH THE RIGHT PROJECT

A student once showed me a hovercraft he was building. For over a year he had been working on the project in a shed, courtesy of the school's maintenance supervisor, who had lent him tools and given advice. As senior year approached, the student knew he'd be busy with the college application process, but he couldn't bear to abandon his hovercraft. He applied for independent study because he wanted to spend less time in class and more on his machine.

I didn't have to ponder whether this student could do the project. He *was* doing it. Decisions about other students are not so easy. Independent study isn't for everyone, though I believe that when the right student works on the right project with appropriate supervision, independent study can be a great option for most. My recommendation is to check with other teachers and counselors who know the student before accepting or rejecting a project. Ask whether there are any problems that might interfere with the student's work. If issues surface, don't give up too quickly. Independent study is fairly adaptable, as this list of common problems and suggested solutions reveals:

- *Disorganized approach to learning.* Help the student formulate frequent, interim goals. Provide a grid, such as the sample provided in Appendix B, to track progress. What will you do during the first week? The next two? Before Halloween? The schedule will evolve, of course, because learning shouldn't be constrained by a preordained path. Students may exceed their weekly quota or fall behind. That's where supervision is key: learning to make and revise a plan is exactly what a disorganized student needs. For students likely to be overwhelmed by a full independent study, you might suggest courses that offer short-term independent projects. (See Chapter 7 for more on incorporating independent study projects in a traditional class.)
- *Spotty attendance record.* Find out why. If absences are the result of illness, independent study work can be scheduled around doctor's appointments and the student's physical condition. If the problem is rebellion or disaffection, consider this definition of independent

study, formulated by a participant years ago: "Independent study is when you get credit for doing what you used to get in trouble for doing when you were supposed to be doing your homework."

- **Disciplinary issues.** See above definition! If that doesn't ease your doubts, speak frankly with the student. An example: "In evaluations, several teachers wrote that you ignore or challenge their instructions. Tell me what you expect from your mentor." A student who shrugs away the conversation—the physical expression of "I don't need a mentor"—may not be ready for independent study. One who answers it honestly, on the other hand, may find a rare success in the course. Plus, the student may learn an important life skill: how to work productively with an authority figure.

- **Poor grades.** Why? If the work has been too difficult, check the level of the proposed project and see whether it is within reach. If not, discuss possible revisions. If it is a question of learning style, independent study is the solution, not the problem. As Avram Schlesinger, the current director of the program at Horace Mann, commented, "This course is not only about students studying a topic of their own interest, but also about students studying in the way they are comfortable." A student who learns best by manipulating objects can design a hands-on project. Visual learners can create wall charts, websites, or videos to show what they have learned.

- **Poor skills.** Be honest with the student about which skills need improvement. Refine the proposal so that strengthening those skills is baked into the methodology and goals of the project.

- **Time management issues.** Help the student map out a counter-schedule. The scheduling grid provided in Appendix B helps here, with two additional columns, one for out-of-school events (a sister's wedding, glee club regionals, and so forth) and one for assignments in other courses (tests, papers, portfolios, and the like). With this visual map, students can see which weeks are heavy with commitments. They can adjust their independent study workload accordingly, spending extra time on their projects during relatively light weeks.

The issues listed above are significant, but more worrisome is a student who wants to do an independent study project—any independent study project. Topic? Not sure. Area of focus? Shrug. Goal? Um . . . Experience tells me that some kids in this category want independence, but they have had so little they don't really know what it feels like. They seem to be asking, "What do you want me to want?" Others think that an independent study project will improve their profile when they apply to college. A legitimate project probably will; a label pasted over a feeble effort will not. In both situations, try to dig beneath the surface to encounter the real human being and then to unearth that person's innate desire to learn. If you and the student can get to that level, other problems may fall away. After all, you can't learn to be independent until you take a stab at it, and everyone is interested in *something*.

One last tip: After I have read the proposals, communicated with those who know the students and with the students themselves, I give a secret test to any kids I am still unsure about. I assign a small task they must complete. For example, I might ask the student to look for an article and print out a copy for me. A student who follows through gains my confidence. One who does not confirms my doubts.

SPOTLIGHT:
Extending an Invitation

"He said, 'You'd be a great person to do this.' I felt so honored!" The *he* is the teacher originally scheduled to run the independent study program at my school. (Before the course began, he accepted an administrative post elsewhere.) The *I* is Emily, who at the time was a high school junior. "He suggested that I do a project on heroes during my senior year, something like 'the invention of the hero in literature.' So I enrolled in the course," Emily told me, "and then you suggested a different topic when you took over the class."

So I did. Contrary to just about everything I have written in this book about students' interests leading the way, I must admit that some excellent projects, like Emily's, arise from teachers' recruitment of candidates for independent study. Here's the thing: some students are obviously going to flourish in an independent setting. They are self-motivated, hardworking, creative, and intellectually curious. Yet independent study may not be their first thought as they select courses. If you know a student like that, why not reach out with an invitation? Recruitment, I must caution, should stay on the "Have you ever thought about . . . ?" level. Any sort of pressure would be wrong for a host of reasons. But a low-key suggestion can open a door to independent study, and a mind to new possibilities.

Having been Emily's academic adviser and English teacher, I knew that she was a good close reader, able to pick apart a text and appreciate levels of meaning. I also knew that she was curious about gender roles and the way in which our understanding of them has evolved. Hence, I suggested a topic that would provide a wealth of material: American literature of the 1950s, 1960s, and 1970s. I knew Emily would run with it—and she did. Together we created a reading list that included Sloan Wilson's *The Man in the Gray Flannel Suit*, all three of John Updike's *Rabbit* books, as well as works by Ann Beattie, Joan Didion, and Ken Kesey. "The course helped me see myself as someone with competence. I didn't just read and summarize. I read and synthesized and then wrote about my ideas. That was a gift," Emily notes. Now a professor of psychology who mentors student researchers herself, Emily says her role, in part, is "not to demotivate them." *Her* motivation to learn was always there, as was her ability. She just needed an invitation.

THE MENTOR'S ROLE

From experience—either positive or negative—you probably have an image of an ideal mentor. So has the person who agrees to be a mentor, and so has the student. Take a moment to calculate how likely it is that all those expectations match perfectly. Everyone is reading the same book, but not everyone is on the same page. Your job is to put them there. First, communicate your expectations to mentors. The web page of the Frisco school district in Texas is a good example. Frisco's program relies on mentors from the business community. The web page tells mentors the time commitment (one hour per week plus two evenings a year) and duties (to invite students to their workplace to "shadow and observe," to "guide them in their studies and advise them on major projects," and to complete five online assessments and evaluate the student's work and year-end presentation). You can also explain the mentors' duties at a faculty meeting or in one-on-one conversations in the teachers' cafeteria.

Students, too, need to know what a mentor does and what their own responsibilities are in the mentor–student relationship. In my school, students receive a handout reminding them that mentors are volunteering their time "out of graciousness, love of our students, and excitement for the opportunities the program creates for each of you." They're directed to "be thankful and cognizant of the time" that mentors give them, and they're told that they should treat mentor meetings as a class, bringing their notes and books or whatever they're working on, arriving on time and ready to work. If they are unavoidably absent, they are told to notify the mentor and reschedule, well in advance if possible.

All these concrete explanations are good, but they don't touch upon perhaps the most important element of mentorship—the changed roles of teacher and student. A mentor isn't teaching a course to a class with one student. Jordan describes the mentor–student relationship this way: "The paradigm is 'I'm going to walk with you while you figure it out.' That model breaks from the usual prescriptive approach. It's a profound gift of humility from the teacher and gives the student a way to transition to the full independence of an adult." Ruthie cites the exhilaration of "trying to solve a problem that my teacher didn't even know the answer to. It was a feeling of teamwork. He had all this math experience, all this knowledge, and he was willing to do research along with me." She adds, "I think this project laid the foundation for my decision to earn a doctorate. So much confidence came from having a mentor who was really invested in my work!" Emma, who wrote a young adult novel for her independent study project, agrees: "The main idea of independent study is that it really *is* independent. I'm pretty good at holding myself accountable." Nevertheless, having a mentor was important to Emma. "It was exciting to talk with someone about my work, someone who really wanted to know what I was doing, who would read what I wrote every week and react to it."

Mentors also provide context for the student's research and act as a sounding board for ideas. They suggest different approaches, name sources they have found valuable, and evaluate sources students have found on their own. They encourage students to take on challenges but also point out limits. Darin Lewis, who has mentored many music projects, remarks, "I might look at someone's composition and say, 'You can't have the violin play E because it doesn't exist on the instrument' or check a research hypothesis and say, 'No one else thinks that, so you are going to have to test your idea carefully and provide evidence.' The mentor's role isn't to stifle but to help the student figure out how to do something better."

In my school, mentors and their students meet once a week. Other schools specify "at regular intervals" and leave it up to the mentor to decide what is necessary. The meetings may last a full period, but they are organic: if the work can be accomplished more quickly, the meeting ends. (Wouldn't you love to see the same principle applied to faculty meetings?)

FINDING MENTORS

It is possible for one teacher to act as mentor to an entire group of students. (If that is your situation, turn to Chapter 4.) In most programs, though, other adults are involved. As director, I mentored about a third of the independent study projects myself, because independent study replaced two of my other classes. For the rest, I reached out. This is where:

- *faculty whose subject area relates most directly to the project* They bring expertise to the meetings, a breadth of knowledge no student can attain in a single independent study. For interdisciplinary projects (more on these in Chapter 5), two teachers can tag-team it, alternating meetings with the student and sharing the task of evaluation.
- *faculty from other disciplines* Academia artificially unravels and sorts threads of knowledge, but real people—and true education—are more complicated. A historian may also be a science fiction writer, a guidance counselor, a gourmet chef. At a faculty lunch I once described a student's plan to build a guitar. He wanted to carve the wooden frame and design the circuitry himself. "I wonder where I can

find someone to mentor that project," I mused. An art teacher shot me a look: "Is that a trick question?" It turns out that building guitars was his hobby. I had no idea! Moral of the story: spread the word about projects that lack mentors. You never know who will volunteer.

- *staff* The maintenance department, cafeteria workers, and security guards have a lot to offer. I have paired projects involving engineering, food, and criminal justice with mentors drawn from their ranks. Not only do these mentors provide expert help, they also challenge students' preconceptions about who can teach.

- *administrators* They are busy, no doubt, but often willing to take on a project. Talking with an enthusiastic student is more appealing than dealing with a boring pile of purchase orders or a complicated disciplinary case. Do not limit yourself to academic administrators. For one project on investment, the school's financial officer stepped in.

- *former faculty and staff* I stepped away a while ago from the daily grind of full-time teaching, happy to be free of papers to grade and administrative forms to fill out. I still love teaching, though, so I am eager to mentor independent study projects. I doubt I am alone in this sentiment. Tap into the school's retiree network, emphasizing that mentor work can be done remotely.

- *alumni* A directory of graduates and their careers is an excellent resource. Alumni are often pleased to return to their school, either virtually or in person, or to have students come to their labs or studios or offices.

- *community resources* Check business and professional associations in your area to see who is willing to mentor. Also talk to someone active in the parents association. In short, network!

Note: Anyone directly employed by the school has almost certainly gone through a background check. Alumni and members of the community probably have not, and retirees may need an update. Check your school's policy to see what is required. It is also a good idea to meet with mentors from outside the school before you sign off on a partnership. If possible, sit in on the first meeting between the mentor and student and monitor the project closely thereafter.

In my school, students may request a specific person to mentor the project, but they are not guaranteed their preferred partner and are told not to approach anyone directly. This policy protects the mentors. Frequently, the same teacher's name appears on multiple proposals. Accepting all requests imposes too heavy a burden, given that meetings take place during the mentor's free time. A faculty-to-faculty conversation allows the requested mentor to accept one project and decline the others without embarrassment.

You may think that it is hard to find mentors. Everyone is busy, and independent study is an add-on. However, my experience is that teachers are keen to work with an enthusiastic student on a project in their field. Or outside it! For many mentors (including me), the chance to learn something new is enticing. I once mentored a project on the Chinese Cultural Revolution. I had only a vague understanding of the topic when Nia and I started, but an expert in Chinese history gave us a reading list and offered to consult as needed. So Nia and I plunged in. Working our way through the books, we kept a running list of questions. One was particularly vexing. Neither of us remembers what the question was, but we both remember catching sight of each other in the hallway one day. She had unearthed the information, and so had I. We ran toward each other, both shouting, "I found it!" The shared joy of that moment more than made up for time spent reading. Janet Smith, a computer teacher who has mentored many students, sees another benefit. "At least five projects led to curricular professional development," she notes. She shows videos of past projects to her current computer-programming and robotics classes, to inform and inspire her students.

SPOTLIGHT:
"Another Layer of Purpose"

"It gives you another layer of purpose when you find a motivated person and watch them grow," says Peter Montesino, who mentored Donavan's independent study in music sampling. When Donavan was in high school, Montesino worked as an audio-video technician and thus spent a lot of time in the school's music studio. So did Donavan, who says that although Montesino was "never my teacher, he was the person who taught me the most at our school." Donavan's project involved "sampling"—taking something from an existing song and changing it to create a new sound by speeding up or slowing down the beat, changing the pitch, looping a phrase, and so forth. Montesino gave Donavan technical help: "how to utilize the tools" of software and equipment. Perhaps even more valuable was the context Montesino provided: "We took a deep dive into the history of hip hop," the music genre closely associated with sampling. "Donavan didn't know its roots were in the culture of Jamaica," he says, "even though his family came from there. The music lit a fire in him." That fire has not gone out; for his job with an audio software company, Donavan uses the skills he learned from Montesino. He continues to compose his own songs and to act as a producer for other artists' work.

Both Montesino and Donavan gained more than skill from the independent study project. "I had the opportunity to show that I can mentor, that I had real-world experience working with students," says Montesino, who now works as an audio-visual technician at a university. The project taught Donavan that "work doesn't have to be terrible." He explains, "I was a bad student: bad at math, bad at science, bad at paying attention." The value of his project, he says, was to know that "I can be good at something and share something I feel talented at." Donavan, who calls Montesino "a Renaissance man who knew how to do a little bit of everything," now often mentors younger musicians. "He never said 'that's trash' if he didn't like something. He kept an open mind. Now when I hear something I don't like, I call it 'interesting and challenging.' I help them understand the core tenets of what makes a song good, and we go from there."

SUPPORTING MENTORS

There is room for variety, of course, but a mentor–student relationship, like any relationship, occasionally requires negotiation and adjustment. A mentor who talks for forty-five minutes out of a fifty-minute period needs to step back a bit. On the other hand, a mentor who says, "Everything good? Okay, see you next week!" needs to step forward, with questions, observations, and suggestions. In the same way, students who view every comment from their mentors as a denial of the "independent" part of independent study have to listen and admit they have something to learn, just as passive students have to speak up and take some control. Most mentor–student pairs find the right level themselves. If they do not, initiate separate conversations with each half of the pair and then make some suggestions. Diplomatically, of course.

The goal is to allow the mentors to experience all the joy and none of the hassle of teaching. Other ways to support the mentors' work include the following:

- securing copies of books and materials for the mentor
- solving scheduling problems
- meeting once every two weeks with students mentored by others—a good way to catch problems as they arise
- working with students as they plan and practice for their presentations, so the mentor doesn't have to
- discussing grading criteria, if the mentor wishes (more on this below)
- taking care of official documentation
- serving as "the designated bad guy" if the student has behaved inappropriately

Crucial to success in independent study, for both mentor and student, is communication. Ideally, they discuss problems as they arise, but the seminar leader has a role here also. An illustration: early on in my role as independent study director, a self-possessed, "I've got it covered" sort of young man was working on a computer project. Well, actually he was *not* working. Swamped with college applications and other courses, he had put his project aside. As seminar leader, I met with him every other week. He arrived empty-handed for a meeting, but he drew an elaborate flowchart illustrating what his code was designed to do. Two weeks later, the same thing happened. I made a mental note to check in with his mentor. I was busy, though, and forgot about the student—until his mentor called to report that he had not seen any work for six weeks. It wasn't too late for the student to catch up—and he did so—but there were hard feelings all around. The mentor was rightly annoyed; he had signed on to help a student he believed was committed to the project. I was annoyed with the student, but most of all with myself. I should have been more careful. After that experience, I requested that all mentors notify me immediately if things were not proceeding as they should be. I also changed my approach. I schedule any student who "left the work at home" for an appointment the following day. That usually elicits a flurry of activity or a more honest account of what work has actually been completed.

ASSESSING PROJECTS

Hand me a stack of essays and I can plunge right in, underlining errors and writing comments. Tell me to pluck a letter for those essays from the standard quintet (ABCDF) and I can do that, too. It is easy to compare (and therefore grade) student efforts when they are all doing the same task. But independent study projects are, by definition, unique. You cannot assess the relative merits of a painting by looking at a research paper or a mathematical proof. Forget about apples and oranges: grading independent study projects is more like comparing apples to lawnmowers.

And yet they must be graded. Some schools use a pass/fail system, which can work just fine and causes a lot less angst. In my school, though, precise evaluations are required. The course grades reflect students' work on their projects and in seminar. (I discuss seminar grading in Chapter 3.) The "project" grade is a holistic assessment of the product—the concrete expression of knowledge or creativity—and the process—how students have challenged themselves and stretched their abilities.

Some advice on project grading:

* *Compare the product with the best version of itself.* Paging Plato! Envision the ideal form of whatever product the student has come up with. Whether it is a paper or an exhibit or a musical score or a chemical analysis, ask how it could be improved. What is beautifully complete and what is missing? What works? What does not?

- *How far has the student come?* Think of the student at the beginning of the grading period and then at the end. How have the student's abilities developed? Is the student better informed, more careful at selecting sources, more skilled at communicating ideas? More daring in artistic expression? Were there missed opportunities?
- *Reach out to other mentors.* The seminar leader sees all the projects, but individual mentors do not. I offer mentors the chance to talk about possible grades and, if requested, share other students' products and describe the work that went into them.
- *Require a detailed self-evaluation.* A student's self-evaluation gives you a framework for your own thoughts. A short sentence ("I worked hard and wrote a good paper") tells you nothing, nor is it helpful to the student. Ask students to list everything they did and to discuss what they learned. They can stop short of assigning themselves a letter grade, and even if they do specify a grade, you can overrule it.

Working one-on-one with a student can be intense, and assigning a grade is thus more difficult. You have seen the struggle, and you should give the student credit for that process. But you must also look at the product dispassionately. When you find it hard to make a decision, turn to a colleague for a fresh perspective. If you have time, compose an evaluation detailing what was good and where improvement is needed.

One more thing about assessing projects: don't measure what the student has done in relation to what appears in the student's proposal. Yes, everyone signed off on a proposed project—the student, the mentor, and the school. You all heaved a sigh of relief because everything was settled. Except nothing is ever settled. Learning changes the learner; creating art changes the artist. Acknowledging that fact, even celebrating it, honors the work the student has done and opens the door to new ideas and perhaps to a new direction for the project.

An example: one young man proposed a study of public housing, first in New York City and then around the world. He selected a project not far from the school and gathered statistics on residents' employment, income, education, and the like. He wrote a fine paper, ten or twelve pages long, on the demographics of public housing. It was submitted, read, discussed, and returned. It "counted" as part of his grade. The next step, according to his proposal, was supposed to be an investigation of British "council houses" during the second marking period. But the student's research had awakened his curiosity about the human beings behind the numbers. So he stayed local, visiting the apartment complex and interviewing residents. That is how he discovered a dearth of public transportation, a serious problem in a city heavily reliant on subways and buses. He wanted to know more: Who had selected the housing site? Where did residents work and how long was their commute? How did these factors affect the jobs they could apply for? He unearthed his "finished" paper, incorporated the new information, and rewrote the conclusion. The resubmitted paper was now about twenty pages long. Before the year ended, it would reach forty pages as he investigated "food deserts" and other quality-of-life factors. Had I measured him by his stated goal at the beginning of the project, the grade would have been low and in no way commensurate with the amount and quality of the work the student did.

To be clear, I would not allow a student to shift topics completely (and I would penalize anyone who did so without permission). A student who begins the year with a biochemistry project can't switch to a survey of mystery novels because "I just read this awesome book." That's not freedom to explore. It is license to follow a whim, the polar opposite of what you want to see in an independent study project, which is commitment to in-depth exploration. In a case like this I would insist that the student stay on topic, though I might suggest applying biochemical principles to a fictional crime-scene investigation and assessing the science content of the result.

When I began directing the independent study program, I thought the project–student–mentor connection was the core of the course. And in some ways, it is. But the heart of the course beats elsewhere—to be precise, in the seminar. That's the subject of the next chapter. Even if your school's program doesn't have a seminar, I hope you will read Chapter 3. Maybe I will convince you, and you can convince those in charge, to establish an independent study seminar.

A slide from Rosy's presentation on the ethics of gene editing and its potential impact on marginalized communities.

The Seminar

He sat across from my desk, nervously running through his lesson plan, which called for a discussion of the short story he had assigned for homework. The plan was well thought out, his questions probing and clear. I smiled to reassure him. "You're all set. I look forward to seeing your class." He nodded. I waited for him to leave, but he did not move. Finally he asked, with a slight quaver in his voice, "What if they don't do my homework? Then what will I talk about?"

As a veteran teacher and administrator, I have mentored a fair number of teachers—experienced educators new to the school and rookies new to the profession. The young man worrying about homework compliance was as rookie as it gets: a seventeen-year-old about to make his first presentation to the independent study seminar. One of the many positive aspects of independent study reveals itself in a moment like this. I like to think the student gained a little more compassion for the hardworking teachers in charge of his education, now that he had become one himself.

I've described one student in this anecdote, but nearly all independent study participants at my school have expressed similar worries when they prep for their first presentations. Learning how to explain ideas and share information is a skill, one we educators work on—and with—all the time. But while independent study presenters lack training, they do have an important advantage: they are teaching their peers, who want them to succeed, if only out of self-interest. It is a short step from "What if they don't do my homework?" to empathy. Plus, as one independent study participant put it, "I'm interested in what you're interested in *because* you're interested in it." Delight in learning is contagious.

Delight in learning, of course, can arise within a variety of formats. For descriptions of how to reap the rewards of seminar without having one, or one of a different design, turn to Chapter 4.

PREP TALKS

To prepare students for their presentations, I talk with each seminar member individually, often a couple of times, as their presentation dates near. I use the questions below as prompts. (If this is too ambitious for your schedule, post the questions in an online document and have students fill in the answers. You can review a bunch at a time and offer a verbal response at the beginning of class.)

- *What do you want the class to learn?* Their initial response is likely to be vague. Press them to make a list of specific points. Emphasize that in one period they cannot teach everything they have learned. (If they can, they have not done enough work.)
- *Which concepts are most important?* Identifying priorities helps them distinguish between what they must include and what is interesting but nonessential. I encourage them to think of their lesson plan as a set of modules. They should decide ahead of time what they can skip if time is running short. They can always backtrack to a topic at the end of the session, if any time remains.

- *What teaching method makes sense?* Many migrate automatically to presentation software—PowerPoint and the like—but prompt them to consider other techniques, such as a discussion or an activity. You may have to help them match the format to the material. For example, the class can discuss something that touches upon common knowledge but not a specialized topic they know nothing about.
- *Will you need any special equipment or material?* This is not a glamorous question, but it is perhaps the most important one on the list. Students sometimes get so caught up in what they want to do that they overlook practical considerations, like the need for a class-sized set of scissors and enough paper for an interactive art project. They need to make a list, which you need to check—twice!
- *How will you divide up the time?* Guide them to a feasible plan: twenty minutes for a group discussion should be enough; five minutes probably is not. Remind them to leave time for questions, or in the case of an activity, for cleanup and storage of materials.
- *Will you assign homework?* It is not necessary, but it may bring their topic into focus before the presentation. Be sure the homework is not too time-consuming, because the focus of independent study should always be on individual projects. Reading a poem or a short article, filling out a survey, or writing a paragraph are reasonable requests. Note: you are the one who checks that the homework is done, not the student. They are teaching, but you are the authority.
- *How will you acknowledge sources?* Because it is an event, not a paper, students sometimes do not realize that they have to cite their sources. Not to do so is plagiarism. Students may list sources on a presentation slide or on a paper handout, or post them on the class website. How they do so does not matter, so long as they give proper credit.

Appendix B provides a handy sample form to help students prepare for their presentations. This form also works well in schools where, instead of an ongoing seminar, there is a capstone presentation at the end of the year or semester. The dates the kids fill in will be different ("two months before" instead of "two weeks before" for large events, for example) but the result is the same. The students organize what they intend to say and do, and the form reminds them to secure everything they need (from technology to posterboard) ahead of time.

SPOTLIGHT:
The Value of Failure

Things don't always go according to plan, but explaining *how* things haven't gone to plan can become the new plan. That is what Wontaek learned the night before his presentation. He had been building a robot, his fourth, aiming to "astound my mentors and even myself." Tinkering with his creation—"the bot was supposed to be perfect"—the young engineer accidentally fried the circuitry. Only a few hours remained before his presentation. "I salvaged what I could," he said. As his classmates watched him put the less-sophisticated robot through its paces, Wontaek explained what had gone wrong with the original model and why. He concluded the presentation by explaining the design of his next robot, which eliminated the problem he had been trying to fix and protected the wiring from overload. Wontaek learned a lot about programming and computer technology from his project, but an important takeaway from the experience of giving a presentation was that "there is always going to be that moment when you mess up, and you learn to be okay with it and to gain something out of it." He now works in software engineering, where part of his job is to "explain tech things to nontech people." Including what went wrong.

Once they have a plan, I offer teaching tips:

• *No matter how carefully you plan, the timing will be off.* A point they assumed would take two minutes to cover gives rise to a question and then to another question and before they come up for air, fifteen minutes have elapsed. (To help with pacing, I quietly signal the presenter at the halfway point, three quarters of the way through, five minutes remaining, and so on.)

- **Stop when you are done.** It doesn't happen often, but sometimes presenters complete their planned lessons early. Perhaps they didn't prepare enough material or rushed through everything. These are problems worth addressing in your evaluation, and you should revisit them as the presenter readies the next presentation. But if the lesson is over, it is over. Filling up time with useless chatter is not helpful; stopping is.

- **In a discussion, be patient.** They throw out a question. The minutes tick by and no one raises a hand. No one is going to, ever. That's how inexperienced teachers feel, but in the real world maybe ten seconds have passed. To keep them from jumping in too soon and answering their own questions, I advise presenters to bring a glass of water to class. A sip after a question keeps the presenter quiet while classmates formulate their responses.

- **Be flexible.** If a discussion is valuable, the presenter can jettison a low-priority item and let comments continue. It is also okay to end a discussion that students prefer to extend. I suggest saying something like "I will go back to that if we have time, but right now we have to move on."

- **Don't panic if there is a technical glitch.** First, there is always a technical glitch. Second, almost always there is a way around the technical glitch. Encourage students to make a backup plan while preparing for the presentation, which I think of as the suspenders-plus-belt approach. If one does not work, the other will save the day. Also remind them that even if the day is not saved, all is not lost. Presentations can be rescheduled because of illness, fire drills, finicky computer connections, and every other annoyance the universe throws at us.

- **Admit that you do not know everything.** "I will find out and let you know" and "I have not studied that" are not only acceptable but expected answers when the class is asking questions. I began including this point in presentation prep after I witnessed a panicked student make up an answer.

- **Do not disguise a lecture as a discussion.** One of my pet peeves is a discussion question that is not a question at all, just a hook dangled over the group until someone comes up with the "right" answer. A question posed to spark interest is fine: "Do you know how many trees there are in Greenland?" Asking "What motivates this character?" and accepting only the answer the presenter has in mind is *not* fine. Remind rookie discussion leaders that they have to listen to what students say and consider all plausible ideas. Also remind them that they do not have to respond to every comment with one of their own. They can call on several students before saying something.

- *Don't overcrowd presentation slides.* How often have you stifled a groan during a meeting because the slides are filled with text, which the presenter reads, word for word? It is fine to present graphic elements or a bulleted list that focuses attention on key points. For everything else: talk!
- *Stay calm.* Okay, calm-ish may be the best some students can hope for. It helps to remind students, as one seminar leader does, that "although presentations are daunting, you are the person who knows more about the topic than anyone else in the room."
- *Pay attention to all.* Urge the presenter to call on as many people as possible, not just the first person to raise a hand. If students are working in small groups, the presenter's role is to drift from one cluster to another or to visit breakout rooms on a virtual platform. The presenter listens for a couple of minutes and comments if appropriate.

No matter how well you prepare students, things can go awry. You are the professional in the room. If someone is unfair or unkind, step in. Be especially vigilant if students are presenting their work at a learning fair or in a community-wide symposium. Discuss possible responses to uncomfortable moments ahead of time, and be sure students know how to contact you or another adult if someone responds inappropriately to their work.

FEEDBACK

Receiving constructive feedback helps students improve their presentations. So does giving it. This is why asking students to evaluate others' presentations is a good idea, as long as you structure the format properly. A vague request for feedback yields vague answers: "It was great!" or "I loved it" or "Are you always this boring?" None of these responses are helpful and the third is hurtful. How is the presenter to understand what worked and what did not? A better path is to ask specific questions, such as these:

- Was sufficient background covered to allow you to understand the topic? If not, what additional information would have been helpful to you?
- Had time permitted, was there a topic you wanted to hear more about? What related topic do you wish had been included? Was there a topic that could have been discussed more briefly?
- What are two things you learned from this presentation?
- What two questions would you like to pose to the presenter?
- Was anything unclear? If so, what?
- What improvement would you suggest the presenter make for next time?

You can ask every student to evaluate the presentation or select a representative sampling. The evaluations should be signed and submitted to you, so you can summarize the results for the presenter, adding a dose of diplomacy if needed.

SPOTLIGHT:
Virtual Origami

In-person learning had shut down. Reopening would not happen for a while. Not a problem for independent study presenters relying on discussion (to the breakout rooms, everyone!) or slides (share screen, got it). Young people are digital natives, and most teachers know their way around technology, too. But what about a presentation that includes hands-on work? That was the dilemma facing Samuel, who had planned his presentation before the pandemic hit. Samuel loves engineering and origami; the focus of his project was computer numerical control (CNC)—basically, computerized instructions given to a machine. Samuel's goal for the year was to build a CNC machine capable of pre-creasing origami paper. During his first presentation, Samuel wanted his classmates to fold origami patterns so they could better understand what the CNC machine would eventually do. This plan was fine for a class that was physically present, but twenty thumbnails on a screen? Not fine. But where there's an independent study, there's a way. Samuel could not hand out paper, but he could send classmates the dimensions of the paper square they needed and have them cut it themselves. On presentation day, he wedged his phone on a shelf above his computer. The camera on his computer showed on his face and the illustrations he had made. His phone's camera filmed his hands. The view was even better than it would have been in an actual classroom, where twenty kids would have had to vie for a close look. Though Samuel says he was nervous ("I got excited about the subject, went off on a tangent, and started talking super-fast"), his presentation was a success.

GRADING

In a perfect world, you would not have to assign grades. People want to learn and, given the chance, they do. In the real world, alas, you generally have to select a letter that assesses student work. In my school, both the project and the seminar contribute to the grade (ABCDF), weighted half and half. In other schools, pass and fail are the options. Here I explain my theory of seminar grading; I discuss project grading in Chapter 2.

For seminar, I make a holistic assessment of the amount and quality of work that has gone into the student's presentation. I compare what the student has done to an ideal presentation on the topic. I draw on my teaching experience to assess whether the material has come across clearly, and I invite mentors to attend and ask for their assessment. (I take copious notes to share with mentors who cannot come to the class. I record virtual presentations so mentors can watch later.) I also give credit to the student for all the good things classmates contributed to the presentation—their peers' remarks or activities. After all, the teacher has guided the class toward learning. That should count! Finally, I assess the student's participation in others' presentations. What did the student add to the seminar? That is not an easy question to answer, but it is an important one. The seminar is a little community, and what an individual contributes matters.

SPOTLIGHT:
A Capstone You Can Eat

Veronica had spent the year reading about Italian cuisine and its roots, both biological (crops and animals) and cultural (holidays and traditions). She browsed through cookbooks and tried out recipes, sometimes several times until the dish tasted right to her. As graduation neared, she was ready for her final presentation to the independent study seminar and felt "the absolute joy of not having to write a final paper." Yet in the end, her capstone presentation did in fact involve a paper. To be more specific: she cooked an eight-course meal for her classmates and created a multipage, annotated menu explaining the origin and context of each dish. She does not remember being nervous about the dinner. (I was. I called a chef friend for guidance twice during the evening to be sure we did not end up in the emergency room because of food poisoning.) While I was worrying, Veronica was simply "figuring out a puzzle: how do I get all these pieces of food together and delivered to a table?" She adds, "I felt such a sense of accomplishment that I pulled it off. It was four times as much work, but it felt like fun. If you are lucky enough, you find that in your career—work that does not feel like work."

SCHEDULING

Ceding class time to student presentations relieves you of one burden (teaching) but imposes another (scheduling). You have to find a slot for each presentation, ideally on a day that works best for the presenter. Count the number of class periods during one grading cycle and divide by the number of students. Now you know what you are facing: a deficit or a surplus of presentation slots. Next, ask students to list their preferred presentation dates, taking into account their work in other courses, extracurricular commitments, and family events. In my experience, students' choices arrayed on a calendar resemble a bell curve (flat ends, big bump in the middle). No one wants an early date because they have not learned enough yet. Besides, it is scary to be first! Few want a late date because the end of a grading period is heavy with assignments and exams. That leaves the majority hoping for a middle spot. At this point you may be tempted to throw up your hands and simply shoehorn everybody onto the calendar or determine dates by lottery. I have resorted to these methods sometimes, allowing students to swap dates among themselves later, as long as all traders are willing and they let me know who is presenting when. Mostly, though, I try to be accommodating. Here are some tricks for solving deficit and bell-curve problems:

- *Divide some periods to accommodate more students.* Two students can share a forty- or fifty-minute period. Each has enough time to go through a few presentation slides or to pose one discussion question. If you are working with a block schedule, three or four presentations may fit into one period.
- *Offer an asynchronous option.* Students can record a talk and post it on the class website. Require everyone to sign in and watch the presentation within a designated span of time. To ensure strict attention, have the presenter assign a small task—perhaps a question students must answer about the presentation they have watched. As always, you, not the presenter, should check that homework is done and follow up if it is not.
- *Schedule some presentations during nonclass time.* Some presentation plans require out-of-class hours—a field trip, for example. One presenter guided us around an art museum; another took us to a nearby school to view their eco-friendly, green roof. Concerts and theatrical productions are generally after school or in the evening. But occasionally I have needed extra periods simply because otherwise there would not be enough spots for everyone. I have hosted independent study lunches and dinners and an occasional weekend event. To compensate for taking their free time, I provide food. Lots of food!
- *Coax a couple of students into earlier dates.* Students often elect to do an independent study because of a long-standing interest,

so they have essentially begun their projects before the class commences. Slot these kids into the earliest dates and give them extra praise for trailblazing.

- *Ease a few students into later dates.* Remind them that they can complete preparations for a presentation some weeks before they are due to give it. With the work done, there is less pressure at the end of the grading period.

If you manage to accommodate students who want the middle dates, you may end up with empty slots at the beginning of the course. Use a couple of periods for logistics—meeting times, discussion of class norms, and so forth—and to hone research skills: source evaluation, record-keeping, and citation. Students whose projects involve creation instead of research may squawk a bit ("I'm sculpting! I don't need sources!"). Point out that they will need these skills in other classes and in real life. If an open period occurs at the end, give the class free time for their own projects. Or, group students with a common interest and ask them to run a discussion: those pursuing projects involving self-expression may pose questions about censorship, scientists and historians may explore how data are interpreted, and so forth.

If the course extends over multiple grading periods, as mine does, you have to go through the scheduling headache more than once. It is generally best if each individual's presentations are evenly spaced. Thus a student whose presentation falls early in the first round will likely present early in subsequent rounds. Keep this fact in mind as you create the presentation calendar.

Of course, if your independent study program has a year-end evening or day of presentations, your scheduling job is easier. All you need to do is divide the time and space and put everyone somewhere. Then you have to figure out traffic patterns, room size, number of guests expected, and details like not scheduling twins' presentations at the same time in different rooms. So, on reflection, not easier at all. Just different. I admit that, even though I favor more frequent presentations, I love attending these celebratory events, which represent the culmination of much effort and growth.

Nearly every student I interviewed for this book cited the seminar or the capstone event as a highlight of the independent study program, not because of what they learned from making their own presentations but because of what they learned from others'. Whether presentations take place throughout the year or only at the end, the power of peer learning is undeniable.

CHAPTER 4

A "go-rig" built by Elizabeth, a sixth grader,
for her school's Engineering Event.

Adaptations

I f you have been reading this book in order, by now you know a lot about the independent study program at my school. But you are in your school, not mine. You may have more or fewer kids, a ton of resources or an empty closet, a large group of mentors or no one but yourself. Your students may be younger or older than the high schoolers I have taught, and the teaching time available for independent study may be much shorter (a month) or longer (a few years). None of these factors determine the quality of an independent study program because the core elements—projects driven by student interest, guardrails to keep students on track, and the sharing of knowledge—are not dependent on setting. Properly adapted, independent study can succeed just about anywhere.

In this chapter I describe diverse school-based independent study programs that work well. Homeschoolers, I address your needs in Chapter

6. I'm confident that you can find a model—or craft one—that works where you do.

ONE CLASS, ONE TEACHER: CHOOSE YOUR OWN ADVENTUROUS STUDY

Can independent study work in a single classroom, with one teacher and no extra meetings? Yes! The proof is Caitlin Wood's "Choose Your Own Adventure" course at Urban Academy, a New York City public high school. "It feels like a different kind of classroom," says Wood, comparing the class to her other social studies courses. "There is a different vibe because you are not the center of what's happening." In other words, she is the only official teacher, but she has a lot of help—the kids themselves. "They talk to each other about what they are reading, what is on their screens as they research their topics," she explains. Wood formalizes this collaboration by pairing students whose topics or skills complement each other or whose work habits mesh well. "My partner was a senior," says Isabel, who took the class when she was in ninth grade. "He already had a better understanding of what we had to do, and that was helpful to me." Wood shifts the partners from time to time, so each can benefit from a new perspective. She helps students during class, moving from student to student with comments and questions. "We really get deep into conversation with her about our topic, and it transcends into something more," Isabel remarks. During their free time, students can also reach out to other faculty or outside experts for research material and source suggestions.

Urban Academy prizes inquiry-based learning and requires that students demonstrate proficiency in a number of academic tasks in order to graduate. One of those tasks is a research paper, which many students work on in Wood's course. Not all, though. Those who have already written papers or who plan to write them in another class sign up for her course just to explore a topic that interests them or, perhaps, as a change of pace from the discussion format of other courses. These students may make a film or a visual display to showcase what they have discovered.

A little more than halfway through the semester, all students make a presentation to the class. For the paper writers, it is a chance to articulate and refine their arguments and evidence. For others, the presentation represents a pivot point. These students may switch topics or do further research into their initial topic for the remainder of the course. Presentations can be slide-based, but some choose to speak solely from notes and perhaps show a video clip or play a song relevant to their topics. A few make informational posters. Isabel chose that last option for her presentation on colorism. "I had note cards with some statistics and a few words to remind me what I wanted to say about why I chose these photos," she says. "I was a bit nervous but I really enjoyed being the teacher. We aren't in that position elsewhere. And the second presentation was easier."

Most presentations are about twenty minutes long, but class comments and questions may extend the time. "I ask four students to be prepared to present on a particular date," explains Wood, "but if we get to only three, I save the fourth for the following class."

By the rules of the course, the topic must be "real, something they can research online or from books and primary sources," explains Wood. (If they want to write poetry, a different class will accommodate them. Ditto for science experiments.) Some students come to the course already knowing what they want to do; others decide when they get there. Either way, the first couple of weeks are devoted to formulating a research question and amassing reliable sources. As they dive in, the topic evolves.

In addition to colorism, Isabel researched the history of tattoos and cultural differences in their significance. Here are a few other topics (adventures!) students have chosen:

- ***Soccer (football)*** When the head of FIFA, the international governing body of the game, was accused of corruption, a student investigated what charges were made and what punishment was imposed. That information led to research into other issues: racism in the fan base, pay disparity between male and female players, and so forth.
- ***Vaccinations*** The starting point was smallpox; then the student looked at a recent outbreak of measles and the COVID-19 pandemic. Research into the anti-vaccination movement led the student to consider whether vaccines should be mandatory.

- *Emancipation* After studying the Civil War, a student posed this research question: Did Abraham Lincoln really free the slaves? In addition to online research, the student was given access to a history teacher's files on the subject.
- *History of Afghanistan* Stoning a woman to death—how could this happen in modern times? How did the Taliban, the group responsible for the execution, gain power? To answer these questions, a student read books on Afghan history, followed current reporting, and watched documentaries about the country.
- *Prison System* Reading *The New Jim Crow* and *Assata: An Autobiography*, as well as news articles, a student researched the American prison system, mass incarceration, and criminal justice issues.
- *Postcard* Independent study permits outside-the-box work like this project centered on a 1950s postcard of a woman in a natural setting. The student's research included geology (What are those rocks? How were they formed?) and sociology (Who wrote the message? What was happening in the world when the card was sent?)
- *Cannibalism* This project had the shock factor beloved by teenagers, but the academic content was solid. The student researched cannibalism among nonhuman animals and incidents among humans; the student also read what philosophers such as Michael Sandel have to say about the practice. The research led to a discussion of the legal and moral aspects of cannibalism.

Evaluation of student work is commensurate with the usual school standards, and students may opt to take the course more than once, either continuing research into one topic or switching to another. Wood notes that it is easy to see if someone is falling behind, as she is checking their work constantly during class. Students track their sources on a "reading sheet," with vocabulary words and quotations from their research material, as well as questions about what they have read—all tasks that strengthen reading skills. Wood explains, "Urban is a school that serves students of all different backgrounds and incoming skills." The individualized format of her course permits her to steer each student to sources that are both challenging and accessible. She adds that the course is a boon to students who have been absent for an extended period. "They aren't coming back to find that everyone else is weeks ahead of them," she explains. "It feels easier to catch up if you're working at your own pace." In other words, though it is an adventure, her class is also a safe and educational journey.

The takeaways for a single-teacher program:

- in-class mentoring
- record-keeping in written logs (Wood's "reading sheet")
- collaborative atmosphere
- presentations during class
- outside help as needed

LONG-FORM: IT'S ALL IN THE SCAFFOLDING

The University Liggett School in Michigan takes the long view of independent study—four years long, to be specific—in its Academic Research Program (ARP). According to Head of School Bart Bronk, the program was formed in answer to this question: "How can we make school stop happening to kids and make school start mattering to kids?" The ARP culminates in senior year with an independent study of the student's choice, but it begins in ninth grade, when freshmen take a full-year class in research methods: how to find sources and evaluate them, how to annotate reading material, and how to cite properly. Freshmen learn the "design thinking" approach to complex problems. They are taught to consider the human dimensions of an issue and to brainstorm and test possible solutions. Mini-projects and exercises in ninth grade also build communication and critical-thinking skills, what Shernaz Minwalla, director of the Academic Research Program, calls a "scaffolding curriculum." Ninth graders are already thinking about topics they may want to pursue. They can glimpse their own future at the annual "Celebration of Research," an event in the spring in which seniors present their projects. It can feel a little overwhelming to younger kids, but also inspiring.

In tenth grade, ARP work shifts to a unit in an existing course on United States history, in which students' research centers on place. The year begins with a three-day trip to see ancient petroglyphs and a colonial fort. Later in the year students visit a battlefield from the War of 1812, study the canals at a historic cider mill, and spend time at the Ford

Piquette Plant, the birthplace of the Model T. They also visit the Charles H. Wright Museum of African American History and the Detroit Historical Society. Anything that catches their interest during these trips may become a research subject. They question docents working at these sites, and in doing so learn how to quote and cite information obtained from an expert. The scaffolding continues!

In eleventh grade, the ARP becomes a separate class again. Now they are browsing topics, with skills honed by two years of practice. The school encourages them to read anything and everything to spark curiosity and also to talk with the adults in their lives for research ideas (building, not coincidentally, networking skills). One young student spoke with his baseball coach, who was about to have shoulder surgery. The coach mentioned that the joint might be repaired with artificial spider silk. That conversation ignited the student's curiosity about spider silk, which became the focus of his ARP.

Defining the project is "a messy process, and that's as it should be," says Liz Dann, a science teacher. "You've got choice, and then you've got voice." They also have the scaffolding their teachers have been constructing over the years. The kids no longer ask, "Why do we have to learn this?" They are too busy employing their skills to write a prospectus in which they explain "what their interest is, what their focus is within that interest, and what gap in the academic conversation they would like to fill," explains Minwalla. The prospectus includes an annotated bibliography, their background research, their goals, and the names of experts they will consult.

The senior ARP class is intense. Students write in their research journal during the last fifteen minutes of every class. The ARP teachers give constant feedback, suggesting new sources or avenues to pursue, and other teachers add their expertise to the students' efforts as the students work on their products. "A product can be a piece of music or a visual work, a laboratory experiment, or a teaching opportunity," says Minwalla. Some students intern at an organization related to their project or collaborate with local businesspeople. One young man connected with a new microbrewery and, with the owners' help, examined the brewery's role in the revitalization of Detroit. More important, he saw how he could be involved in that civic effort. Running throughout a high school career, and then beyond: that's long-form independent study at its best.

A sampling of other ARP projects:

- *mental health and wellness for teens* Two projects started with questions: What mental-health issues are common among adolescents? What helps? One project focused on the psychological effects of bedroom design, the other on resources offered by schools. In addition to their written work, the students created a meditation room in their school.
- *gene editing* The student started off as a fan of CRISPR, but research led her to consider the potential downsides of this technique. She combined lab and written work for this project and made a podcast reporting her findings.
- *compressed air vehicle* A student designed and built a go-cart with a compressed-air system that captures the energy of braking and uses it to power the vehicle.
- *urban planning and gentrification* Focusing on neighborhoods in Detroit, the project explored what has changed, what should not change, and why.
- *feminism and science fiction* The capstone of this project was an interactive artwork entitled "How Can Visionary Fiction Installation Art Be a Tool for Feminist Activism by Subverting Subconscious Prejudices Within Audiences?"

The takeaways for a long-form program:

- skills introduced in the first year and reinforced thereafter
- mini-projects each year, with some degree of choice
- student-designed capstone project
- unified approach to research skills in all classes
- display of older students' work to the community

MIDDLE SCHOOL INDEPENDENT STUDY: STOPLIGHTS AND LANES

"Think of a roadway. We have freedom to drive where we wish precisely because we have stoplights and lanes." That is a bedrock principle of

Meredith Olson's approach to the independent work she schedules into grades four through eight at Seattle Country Day School. Olson, "Doc O" to her students, runs the school's annual Engineering Event, which showcases what the children build. It is a joyful event indeed, as the contraptions the children have designed and built speed, limp, totter, and occasionally topple. She has shared her teaching methods with teachers in many schools, commenting, "When it fails, it is because teachers just cut them loose. It is really important that you put a tight enough rein on the inquiry so that children achieve success. With enough framework, with high enough guardrails, they do."

Olson's version of independent study is perfect for the age group she teaches. The children have choice, within limits. She chooses an engineering principle each year for the Engineering Event, often tied to something in the news. When Japan debuted a bullet train in 2020, for example, Olson selected "bogie suspension systems" as a theme. (A "bogie" is a low frame running on two or more pairs of wheels, like a train car.) The first round of the project was entirely teacher-directed. Olson gave every student a banana-split dish to use as a chassis and other items that could be turned into axles and wheels. The kids figured out how to build their "go machine." Then they worked on improving its performance. How could they reduce friction? Increase speed? Navigate better over bumps? The children have some independence at this point, freely experimenting to discover what works and what does not. Ideas flow: anyone who has significantly reduced friction, for example, becomes a "local expert" whom others may consult. In each subsequent round, student independence increases. The teacher sets design targets, but how the kids get there is up to them. They select parts from Olson's trove, which may include popcorn cups, plastic piping, and fidget-spinner bearings. They build at home, too, from whatever material they find there. (Garbage-can wheels, anyone?) During a recent year, one student constructed a chassis strong enough to carry her dog. Others built small vehicles powered by rubber bands or mouse traps. Some rigs worked well, some did not. No worries, according to Olson: "It is not bad that your rig crashed into the table. It just means you have to try something else."

Olson's work is in science and engineering, but the principles under-lying her program apply to other academic areas, too. The takeaways for independent study with middle schoolers:

- challenging but achievable
- structured first steps
- oversight, not control
- safety first
- collaboration, not a contest
- consideration for the whole child

That last point needs elaboration. A young child can be an engineer, but a young child is much more than an engineer. Ditto for historian, artist, or scientist. Ellie Peterson, a science teacher whose students participate in the Engineering Event, checks on her children's wellbeing as she monitors their work. They write reflections in their science notebooks and draw two emojis to represent their feelings, one about their effort and another about their results. "Sometimes, they draw a smile for effort and a frown for results," she says, "or the opposite." A small exercise, but it shows children that their teacher takes their emotions seriously.

COMMUNITY-BASED PROGRAMS: A GLIMPSE OF THE REAL WORLD

"We're going to see changes in the way business is done," remarked Seth Rutledge in early 2021. Rutledge directs the Prosper Career Independent Study program (PCIS) in the public high schools of Prosper, Texas. "With COVID-19, the professional world pivoted." Wherever that world is going, Prosper students will go also, prepared by what the course description calls "experiential learning." I call it a glimpse of the real world, and also an independent study program that turns outward, tapping into the community to secure as many mentors as the kids need.

PCIS classes do have teachers, of course. Their role is to prepare students to work in a professional setting and to ensure that all involved, both mentors and students, fulfill the commitment they made when they agreed to be part of the program. The class is an elective open to juniors and seniors, who must complete a written application and be interviewed about their goals and expectations. When the school year begins, students research their chosen fields during their PCIS class, which meets one block period every other day. While reading about various industries and career paths, they strengthen skills such as critical thinking, evaluation of sources, and note-taking. But PCIS goes beyond academia, exploring these questions and more with students: How do professionals in the field dress? What are the communication protocols in a work environment? What is the etiquette of a virtual meeting or an in-person conference? Research delves into logistics, too. Which nearby companies in their field of interest accept student interns? Whom should the student contact? Armed with lists they have compiled, students make "cold calls" or write emails asking about opportunities that might be open to them, and in doing so, add to their skill set. They also formally share their findings with classmates—presentation practice!

After a month, PCIS sponsors a networking event—"a sort of 'speed-dating' for student interns and mentors," Rutledge calls it. In preparation for the event, he reaches out to invite community leaders, parents, and alumni interested in mentoring. It is a hectic morning but a valuable one, as many students find potential fields of study or mentors. Back in class, they follow up on their leads, once again building a life skill.

"Then they transition to the work itself," Rutledge explains. They may spend their PCIS class time off campus, at their mentor's workplace. Sometimes they miss other classes in order to do so. Rutledge says there are few problems because "they are used to juggling multiple calendars for classes, extracurriculars, and now PCIS."

Where do they go? To an innovative tech company, a university science lab, an exotic animal veterinary practice, a professional soccer stadium, a political campaign office, and many more places. What do they do there? Original, meaningful projects. No one is fetching coffee for the boss! Nor is anyone sitting on the sideline, passively observing. Rather, students become entrepreneurs (some have started businesses), design and construct a drone, assist at a photo shoot, or do other meaningful work. How do students react? One remarked that the class "helped cement my interest in aerospace and made clear my path for the future." Another stated that PCIS had not only "strengthened my knowledge of the medical field but also made me a more confident, professional speaker and individual."

The year culminates in an evening celebration of the projects, to which mentors and parents and other members of the community are invited. To prepare for the event, students give practice presentations to their classmates, who provide constructive feedback—yet another life skill fostered by PCIS. Rutledge and his colleagues in PCIS keep everything flowing smoothly, despite the large number of mentors involved. They problem-solve as needed and do their best to ensure that students' experiential learning is successful.

Not every community-based independent study program is oriented to careers, though workplace skills are strengthened whether that is the intent or not. How could they not be, when students are working with professionals in the "real world"? A few key elements of a successful program with outside mentors:

- networking to build a substantial mentor base
- frequent check-ins through student work logs, emails, or phone calls to mentors, and meticulous attendance records
- attention to logistics (transportation, availability of materials, scheduling)
- respect for the mentors' time and dedication through student accountability
- safety precautions (background checks, monitoring student reactions, and following up on any issues that arise)

All this sounds like a lot of work, because it is. But looking to the community expands your resources immensely, without cost. A welcome side effect is that community members often stay involved with the school. Working with kids taps into people's desire to build a brighter future.

NONCREDIT PROGRAMS: WHAT THEY DO FOR LOVE

No credit, no grades, very little structure. This does *not* sound like a recipe for successful independent study, and sometimes, to be candid, it is not. But when it is, oh my! Magic happens. Jennifer Ward of Michigan's Grandville High School describes the school's MiProject independent study program this way: "You watch the light in their eyes when they have the space and the autonomy to delve into a project they are incredibly curious about. It is a breath of fresh air. When students figure out the direction of their own learning, they see the value of learning itself. *This* is what grows lifelong learners."

The program started a couple of years ago as an option for the school's weekly "seminar" period, scheduled every Wednesday. No traditional classes meet during seminar, which was instituted as time for intervention, remediation, or enrichment. MiProject participants have a self-structured project, "with an action plan and a step list of dates when work will be completed," explains Ward. They also have a mentor, sometimes Ward herself or perhaps another adult in the school community or beyond. "My job is connection," says Ward. "I am always talking about MiProject, reaching out to my friends. I tell them what I am working on, and people often say, 'If you ever have a kid interested in this, let me know.'" Ward keeps a mental list of specialties in the school community that students might not be aware of. She cites an English teacher who plays in a band and has mentored music projects. She is always on the lookout. An industrial designer, a friend, oversaw the work of a student designing and constructing a chair. "Her project was not just drawing," comments Ward. "It was measurement and math, scientific principles, as well as design. Adults tend to silo learning, but MiProject gets us out of that mindset." A few MiProject students write poetry, mentored by a local poetry group, and last year "the symphony kids" played music that Zach, a MiProject participant, composed. "He pulled lots of friends into the project during the two years he worked on it," Ward says. "His band director was the mentor." The flexibility to stay with a project that long—or to drop it if it conflicts with other goals—is valuable. "Sometimes I have to counsel kids out," explains Ward. "Maybe they had a fantastic idea but too many other responsibilities, and their academic work started to suffer. It is all about finding a balance."

Ward helps them with that issue and others during monthly group meetings. "They sit in a circle in the library and bring what they are working on to the group. It is a collaborative conversation. They rely on one another for support," she says. "I am not the expert in the room. I get to learn along with the students, to ask a lot of questions, to pull in anyone who can add something." Ward knows that "it takes a little getting used to, because there is no 'heavy' holding the work over their heads. It is on them. For some, that is empowering." The work culminates in May, when Ward runs what she calls "a TED-like showcase" for MiProject kids. Sometimes there is a bigger audience: poets may publish their work or read a poem during daily announcements, for example.

Grandville students have another independent study option, too. They can seek out a faculty mentor for a one-semester project. Officially, this sort of independent study earns a half-credit, but that is not the true motivation; Grandville students generally graduate with more credits than the school requires. Students propose independent studies for other reasons. Recently, for instance, English teacher Linda Berlin mentored a student who was writing a novel. Berlin explains, "She wanted the time in her schedule blocked off for this purpose. She was not seeking an editor or a writing teacher, and I would not have had time for that anyway. She needed time to write. When we met, she reported her daily word counts. Sometimes we talked about revision strategies or writers' block." Other students seek out this independent study option as a way to go deeper into a topic covered in a previous course. Berlin's World Religions class, for example, sparked two students' interest. "The class was over, but they wanted to learn about religions we had not explored. They covered the same topics—rites of passage, beliefs, and so forth—but in religions that are not part of the curriculum." The students showed their work to Berlin every couple of weeks and returned to World Religions class with a formal presentation, complete with a PowerPoint and traditional holiday foods.

Teachers mentor these independent studies out of "love for learning," both Ward and Berlin agree. They are not paid, and they can always say no. Berlin says she tends to respond with "tell me how you want to do this and I will see how we can make it work." The administration requires an "expression of learning" (a product) to show that the independent study was valid, but that is not what keeps the students going. They, too, do this work for love.

A few takeaways for a noncredit independent study:

- realistic work expectations
- counseling out of some students (over-committed, losing interest)
- student-set benchmarks and interim goals, with faculty input
- mentor and program director as problem-solvers, not disciplinarians

IN THE VIRTUAL WORLD

I think I speak for everyone when I say that I hope we never again face a situation in which schools close for safety reasons and education moves online or goes hybrid (part of the class attending in person, part via internet). But we may. Plus, even without a global emergency, during any given year one or more of your students may need to work remotely because of family issues, health problems, or other reasons. The good news is that independent study pivots easily from in-person to online to hybrid and back again. During intense periods of the pandemic, many independent study programs did exactly that, and the results were generally equal to those achieved in other courses. In many cases, independent study fared better than traditional subjects.

Not surprisingly, good technology and reliable access to the internet are important factors. Yet, as the pandemic made evident, far too many students have neither. The advantage of independent work is the relatively low amount of class time it requires. Thus independent study requires fewer trips to a WiFi hot spot.

I should note that project work may be possible even without the internet. Students who plan carefully can send notes via "snail mail" (on paper, with a stamp). Another alternative is for the school to arrange an independent study mailbox, perhaps outdoors on school grounds, where students pick up or drop off work at set intervals. After each exchange, the mentor and student confer by phone. That is what I did for a few years, long before the pandemic. I was not teaching full-time and, for personal reasons, I could not easily make the long commute to and from school. Each student I mentored called me at a prearranged time, having sent me their week's work the day before. One used email, the other relied on a friend who lived near me to act as our personal delivery system. Both projects proceeded seamlessly. I did go to school to see their presentations, but had I not been able to do so, the seminar leader would have given me a report. (More on presentations in a moment.)

A few other project-related issues arise in virtual and hybrid formats. With a bit of ingenuity, most can be solved. Some problems and solutions:

- *internships* When a work site is closed to visitors, students miss out on a lot. They cannot soak up the office atmosphere or witness interactions between colleagues. There is no opportunity to join informal conversations during lunch or coffee breaks. Nor can they participate in a team experience at, for example, a photo shoot or a sporting event. However, much is still possible in the virtual world. In the same way a manager guides employees working remotely, a mentor may supervise a project. Instead of a weekly visit, the pair meets online or the intern logs into a company meeting.

- *hands-on work* Any project involving specific equipment or designated space may need adjustment if the school or job site is closed. The photographer's assistant can lay out photo spreads or do other postproduction tasks; the sports intern can calculate statistics or analyze videos of past games. In a hybrid situation, students whose projects rely on equipment available only at school or at a work site must take advantage of every available in-person moment (one photo session or sports practice, for example) and then follow up off-site. Samuel, who needed a machine in the school's robotics lab for his project, describes rushing to school to fabricate parts whenever the building was open. At home, he assembled the parts and wrote code. His interim goals and deadlines for the project changed; nevertheless, Samuel accomplished at least some of his primary objectives.

- *performance-based projects* Nothing can replace the energy of a real audience in the room where a performance takes place. However, live-streamed or prerecorded events do have one advantage: more people can see them. During the pandemic, I "attended" a number of grandchild recitals, debates, and open-school days that I had always missed in previous years because of geography. (They live on the West Coast, I on the East.) One important point about performance projects: remember to schedule virtual rehearsals, too.

This can be tricky for ensemble work, but then it is tricky when school is open, too.

Most presentations to the independent study seminar, whether they are performance-based or not, work reasonably well online. A few tips:

- Mandate a rehearsal for any presenter working from home so that technical problems can be tackled before presentation day. The student should have everything ready to go at the rehearsal: slides, audio or video clips, activities, and so forth. You do not want to find out, mid-presentation, that an essential app is *not* on the student's personal computer.
- Discussions involving the entire class can be awkward online. Thumbnail images usually overflow the main screen, and the presenter cannot gauge the class's reaction while seeing only three or four students at a time. For this reason, small clusters of students in breakout rooms are a better choice for discussion-based lessons. The presenter spends a few minutes with each group, and a designated member reports the group's conclusions to the class when everyone reassembles.
- In hybrid situations, sound can be a problem. If only one computer's microphone is broadcasting, the presenter's voice will be clear to those at home, but comments from students in the classroom may be inaudible. A second microphone or computer set in the middle of the room helps. If that arrangement is not possible, encourage students to take advantage of the chat function. Remind everyone to speak clearly and, contrary to everything you usually tell them, in their outdoor, LOUD voices.
- If students make more than one presentation during the course, record the first round and review the presentations with them, pointing out what worked in this format and what did not. Practice may not make perfect in the virtual world, or any world, for that matter, but it will probably make better presenters.
- If presentations usually take place at a single large, in-person event, record them and allow students and guests to view them asynchronously. Or, schedule a presentation week or two, with a few students live-streaming each day.

Entering the virtual world by choice can be liberating. Being pushed there by an emergency is not, at least initially. If you are in this situation, keep this silver lining in mind: being flexible enough to overcome obstacles affords a valuable life lesson to students—and their teacher!

As you see, flexibility—in format, time span, staffing, and budget—is a hallmark of independent study. Whatever your circumstances, you can find a way to make this program work for your students.

CHAPTER 5

Sample panels from David's comic book, a satirical look at the college application process and the product of his year-long independent study.

Subject Area Tips

Picture twenty independent study-ers and one teacher sitting in a classroom with the lights out and thick black paper taped over all the windows. The only illumination comes through a pinhole punched in one panel. On the opposite wall, on a small sheet of paper, students see an upside-down image of the tree outside. The kids are mesmerized by the presentation, as well they should be. The presenter is explaining how a camera obscura works *while they are sitting in one.*

Sounds great, right? The history of photography came so alive in the presentation that the end of the period surprised us all. I rushed off to another class as the presenter promised to return during his lunch break to remove the paper. Within minutes, though, a colleague called me. His class was sweating in the dark room because, well, not much air makes it through a pinhole. Oops.

I learned something about arts presentations from that one: make sure the lesson plan includes cleanup time. An art teacher probably would have known this already, but we English teachers generally just pick up our books and go on our way. Through the years I have learned many other things about independent study projects and presentations, both within my subject area and outside of it. What? Read on.

LANGUAGE ARTS

This is my home ballpark, so I will start here. Students pursuing language arts projects explore literature, create some of their own, or combine reading and writing endeavors. A sampling appears below.

I have mentored many literature and writing projects myself and overseen others as program director. From that experience I offer these tips, divided according to the type of project.

Reading Projects

In this category are projects that survey works by one author, various authors during one time period, or one theme in works from many authors and eras. I could list more variations, but you get the idea: students read. Some issues that arise:

- *student workload* How many pages should a student read each week? That is often the first question the mentor asks, but it is the wrong one: some people read slowly, others quickly. A better query concerns how much time a student plans to devote to independent study reading. I find it helpful to ask how many hours it took to complete a required work from the English curriculum. That gives me an idea of the student's reading speed, after which we can discuss a reasonable number of pages per week.

> plays of Oscar Wilde
> writing a screenplay
> Arthurian legends
> writing a young adult novel
> the sonnet through the ages
> comparing male and female
>   coming-of-age stories
> Langston Hughes's poetry
> religion in Shakespeare's plays
> sci-fi novels of Philip K. Dick
> writing a memoir
> Emily Dickinson's poetry

- *mentor reading* Is the mentor going to read along with the student? I enjoy revisiting old favorites and meeting new writers, so when I am mentoring a literature project I tend to assign myself everything the student is reading. But some mentors do not read along, and the project works just fine. The student annotates (more on that in a minute), and the mentor reacts to the student's comments. Instead of answering questions, the mentor guides the student to dig deeper into the text or to consult outside sources.

- *annotation* If it is a library book, I recommend that students write questions or comments on sticky notes and place the notes on key passages. They write or type the comments at the end of their reading session, each labeled with the page it refers to. If the student owns the book or if it is an electronic source, highlighting is the way to go. To log the work, the student can show the book to the mentor or snap a photo of the annotations.

- *critical reading* Some students find it useful to know what scholars have said about a text. To others, reading literary criticism is like playing the violin with gloves on. This is not a right/wrong issue, but rather something that should be decided as the project proposal develops, with reevaluation as needed.

- *product* Lots of possibilities here: a reading journal, a critical essay, a creative response (visual art, performance, creative writing), or a comparative essay. Interdisciplinary products, such as analyzing the work in the context of noteworthy events or cultural norms of the time, are worth exploring. (More on interdisciplinary projects appears later in this chapter.)

- *presentation* Literature lends itself to discussion, but the class cannot discuss something they have not read. (Yes, I know that some kids do so in traditional classes when they fall behind on the homework assignments. I prefer that independent study aim higher.) The presenter may assign some reading, but not too much. That means choosing a passage and discussing its writing style or characterization or setting. The presenter can also discuss the context of the work and critical reaction to it. Poetry, of course, is easier: a full-period presentation allows enough time for the class to read a poem and discuss it, if the poem is not too long. For drama, the class can act out short scenes and then discuss their interpretations. Plot is usually out of reach, unless the presenter assigns a short story for homework.

SPOTLIGHT:
A Thing That Sparked

Amatullah was searching for connection to her culture, and she found it in her independent study. "I was a Black teenage girl, trying to define my identity within a predominantly white school," she says. "My mom had all these shelves filled with books by Black writers. None of them were in our English curriculum." She turned to independent study, where, she says, "An inner driver powered the work. Independent study was a niche to explore the questions that were bubbling inside me, an incubator where I could grow." Amatullah's grandparents had been part of the Great Migration, moving north to Harlem in the early twentieth century, so her project started with the Harlem Renaissance, many of whose authors took the same journey. She read the novels of Zora Neale Hurston, Jessie Fauset, and Nella Larsen. Then Amatullah moved onward in time with the works of Alice Walker and Toni Morrison, among others. She explored how these writers defined personhood for their Black female protagonists free of and within gendered and racialized structures—powerful stuff for a teenage student. Instead of an analytical literary essay, Amatullah wrote short stories for the product portion of her project. "I was exploring my voice at the same time I was exploring these writers," she explains. "The rigor was still there, but the course allowed me to play with different formats."

As she worked on her independent study, Amatullah spoke to an English teacher about making the required curriculum more inclusive. "Initially, I was told that it would be too difficult to teach or for students to understand, for example, Zora Neale Hurston's books as they incorporated Black southern vernacular. Having found my voice, I replied, 'But we learn Shakespearean English.'" Amatullah became an agent of change, presenting her work at a schoolwide symposium and in other venues. Inspired by her project, teachers selected books that she had recommended and assigned them in their classes. Amatullah remembers independent study as "a course that sparked, and then gave that spark to others." If independent study "sparked," so did she.

Writing projects

I love these, I admit. Novels, short stories, poetry collections, plays, non-fiction of all sorts, plus genre-defying mashups: these are presents I get to open each week when I'm mentoring a writing project, and at longer intervals when someone else is. A few suggestions:

- *the mentor's role* In a traditional class, I may take an active role in explaining what student writers should and should not do, and I teach the conventions of formal English. When I am mentoring, I do not measure writing by an external standard. Instead, I tell the writer what I perceive after I carefully read the work. Whether my remarks reflect or differ from the intended effect gives the writer useful information. I also point out patterns (repetition or passive voice, for example) and nonstandard grammar or punctuation. I ask questions: Why is this character angry? What is the logical bridge between these two ideas? The writer chooses how to respond to my remarks.
- *reading?* Student writers may benefit from reading how-to books, especially for genres they have not previously attempted. Many like to read examples in their chosen genre—a memoirist reading memoirs, a poet reading poetry, and so forth. Others want to stay focused on their own writing. Such options should be discussed during the proposal stage and open to change thereafter.
- *output* The student may commit to writing a certain number of words per day or to completing a draft by a set date. In theory, that is a good idea. No one wants a student to drift around, endlessly planning—and failing—to get something on paper. That said, creative work does not always flow smoothly. Inspiration may strike and

result in a flurry of activity, or it may dry up and result in a frustratingly blank screen. (This I know from my own experience as a writer.) The dilemma, then, is how to hold the student accountable while acknowledging that writer's block exists. My solution, when a student shows me little or no work, is to ask why. If it is a block, I suggest parallel work. Can't write the fight scene? Write something that probably will not make it into the finished work: a description of two characters having coffee, perhaps. Stuck in the middle of a poem? Fine. Write ten metaphors describing the feeling of being stuck in the middle of a poem. You get the idea: I demand production, but not on task. Sometimes that is enough to disintegrate the block. If it is not, at least the writer wrote.

- *presentation* Student writers often distribute excerpts from their work and discuss one or more aspects of style. They may also talk about their writing process and give students a chance to respond to a writing prompt and share the results. Sometimes presenters ask for feedback, work-shopping a piece they have written.

- *publication* Writers need readers, so I encourage independent study authors to submit their work to school and community publications. If there are several writing projects (including creative works and research papers), you can publish a year-end "best of" independent study magazine, either on paper or on the class website. Editing and layout can be part of the project.

- *performance* Poetry and drama projects may find an audience in a school assembly or broadcast. Poetry is usually a solo form, but drama requires actors. Student playwrights may overestimate the amount of time their friends can devote to rehearsing a work, and not everyone may be free when the final presentation is scheduled. Nail down the details as early as possible, and choose alternatives (a single scene, a table-read) if a full performance is not feasible.

FOREIGN LANGUAGE

Linguists who have taken every course or language offered in school and nevertheless thirst for more can expand their language ability through independent study. So can translators, or those who prefer their language study with an extra dose of culture. Some projects with a foreign language focus appear in the sidebar.

Some of the best independent study projects I've encountered have involved foreign-language study, but this subject area does present unique challenges. Some recommendations:

cinema of the Spanish Civil War
Dante's *Inferno*
comparison of French, Spanish, and English-language newspapers
writing and illustrating a Japanese-language children's book
Latin poetry
Welsh language and culture
Ladino and its connection to the Sephardic community

- *language acquisition* It is hard to start from scratch with a new language if you have only one mentor meeting a week, the usual independent study schedule. I encourage such applicants to find a traditional class, or, if none is available, to supplement mentor meetings with a language-learning app such as Duolingo. I also recommend that beginners record their mentor meetings and replay them later, to practice listening and pronunciation skills.

- *advanced study* Building on a solid base is easier, though practice time for oral work may still present a problem. Reading increases vocabulary and reinforces grammar, whether the material is a literary work or newspapers and magazines. E-readers with built-in bilingual dictionaries are helpful vocabulary builders, too. Watching films and news broadcasts or listening to podcasts and radio shows strengthens oral comprehension.

- *translation* Students may translate poetry or other literary works from their first language into the language they are learning, and vice versa. They can focus on connotation and denotation, as well as the limitations of translation—an excellent presentation focus.

- *linguistics* The structure of language itself fascinates some students. One analyzed "conlangs" (languages constructed for a novel or film) and then created a conlang of her own. Another project on historical linguistics focused on Spanish and Portuguese in South America and Europe. Linguistics projects require attention to detail and a good knowledge of grammar, so it is important to screen these projects carefully.

- *culture* For those who are fluent—or fluent enough to get by—watching films, television programs, or news and talk shows can be fascinating and educational. So can a study of traditional foods and celebrations, via written or broadcast material. Visiting a community to speak with residents about their lives is also a worthwhile project. (You should talk with students doing this sort of project about how to handle interactions safely and sensitively. They are talking with people, not "subjects.")

- *writing* Those with a fair command of an acquired language can attempt a writing project in any genre.

- *presentation* For language-learning projects, short vocabulary lessons and perhaps some pronunciation exercises work reasonably well. For intermediate or advanced students, showing a video clip and sharing reading material in translation are good starting points. The presenter discusses the works and their cultural context.

SPOTLIGHT:
Building a Bridge

The ingredients for one amazing independent study project:

a student whose first language was Albanian
a mentor who did not know Albanian but did know Latin
a poem about an Albanian national hero, written in Albanian
a Latin translation of the poem

Atdhe, the student, grew up in Kosovo. He and his family were forced to flee their home in 1999, during the Kosovo War. They made their way to New York City, where Atdhe and his siblings enrolled in my school. When Atdhe joined my English 9 class, he was struggling with the language but progressing at a rapid pace. By senior year he was fluent and ready to stretch his English skills while reconnecting with the culture of his homeland. His independent study project was to translate a sixteenth-century epic about the Albanian hero, Scanderbeg, into English. Atdhe knew much about Scanderbeg but had never read the poem, which was written in archaic language. What a great idea for a project! The only problem was that no one on the faculty understood Albanian, either archaic or modern.

Atdhe was not deterred. He found two copies of the poem in a university library, one in the original language and one in Latin. An English teacher with a good command of Latin was willing to read along with Atdhe. He worked from the Albanian version, she from the Latin. Each week Atdhe wrote a literal translation of a portion of the poem and then, with his mentor's help, polished what he had written. His mentor later reflected that the project showed how Atdhe was "deeply connected to the world which he had been forced to flee but interested in bridging the gap between that world and his newly adopted home." Atdhe's sister, Gresa, followed in her brother's independent footsteps by reading about the history of Kosovo and constructing a massive timeline installed in a school hallway. She also collected and translated some oral histories from others who went through the war. Atdhe's and Gresa's projects served as a link between two cultures for them, and also for their classmates and me.

STEM PROJECTS

The STEM fields (science, technology, engineering, and mathematics) attract a lot of attention these days, and a lot of independent study proposals, too. To illustrate the wide array of possibilities, the sidebar lists some projects students have done through the years:

Their educational value of STEM projects is easy to see, but sometimes the logistics are not as obvious. A few observations appear below.

building a robot
coding an app
engineering principles of bridge construction
non-Euclidean geometry
Asperger Syndrome
perpetual-motion machines
algae biofuel
the mathematics of fashion
statistics of cancer research
Leonardo da Vinci and science

Science

• *fieldwork projects* These require administrative and parental permission if the student leaves school grounds, unaccompanied or chaperoned, during or after the school day. Most important: check the project design to be sure that it is safe, in terms of location, activity, and human interactions.

- *lab projects* Space is a prime issue here. Be sure to check that the room where the student plans to work is free when the student is and that there is a secure place to store materials. Experiments that continue while school is on break pose another challenge. Who is going to feed the critters? Clean the tanks or cages? Nail down all these details before you accept a proposed lab project.

- *research from written sources* This sort of project is simpler to organize, and with the internet, more accessible. Remind students to look for government data on the topic (tax dollars at work!) and to investigate PLoS, a nonprofit, open-access, online trove of scientific papers. Whenever students refer to sources, in their notes or presentations, require that they specify the date of publication, because scientists build on the work of other scientists, correcting and refining conclusions as more data come in.

- *science presentations* Generally, the factors that make field and lab work difficult make presentations exciting. Just be sure the lab is available if a student plans to hold class there. Do not show up with twenty kids, as I once did, for a physics presentation only to discover a biology class in full swing. Also check the student's lesson plan. Specialized vocabulary may roll easily off the tongue of someone who has been using it daily, but these terms tend to befuddle everyone else. A handout or presentation slide or a list on the chalkboard helps, especially if the terms are defined in ordinary language. If the topic is one the class knows little about, encourage presenters to explain the broad concepts underlying the details they've discovered.

Technology and Engineering

Technology projects (anything to do with computers, robots, apps, and the like) can be hard to explain to non-techies, as can engineering projects (bridge design, bionic limbs, maglev vehicles, and so forth). The big advantage is that these projects tend to have fun toys. Sometimes literal toys: to illustrate its construction, a student once dissected a Furby, a furry little creature programmed to respond to voice commands and location. He showed the Furby to the class, explained how it functioned, and put it through its paces. Then he placed it under the desk while he discussed elements of the coding. His serious intellectual statements were punctuated every minute or so by "it's dark here" or "play with me" from the Furby. It was hard to concentrate, to say the least, but we never forgot the lesson either.

Here are some tips for tech and engineering projects, both toyful and toyless:

- ***tech projects*** Developments in this field are fast and frequent. A computer language that is cutting edge in the spring may be passé by winter. Fortunately, mentors in the field tend to be flexible, and independent study expectations should be as well. Products for this sort of project may be lines of code, computer-controlled devices, student-created apps, and the like. Keeping a work log is important because a technical problem at the last minute can ruin the intended product. To evaluate process, the mentor needs to see it.

- ***engineering projects*** These can be purely theoretical, with students poring over schematics or reading reports on stressors and durability of building materials. Or they can involve models, such as the 3D-printed prosthetics that one student designed. Materials for models can be expensive: check the recycling bin first, for the sake of your budget and the environment. Also call local businesses for leftover scraps that would otherwise be discarded or for access to equipment not in use. Safety is an issue whenever students are building something; I rely on the maintenance staff for advice.

- ***presentations*** Computers crash. Robots fry. All sorts of other horrible things can happen during a presentation involving tech or engineering models. Be sure students have a plan B (maybe plans C and D also) if problems arise. One example, from years ago when networks had limited capability: a student was showing the seminar how to play a game he had designed. As he began, his classmates' fingers hovered over keyboards, waiting for him to say "enter" so they could push that key. He did, they did, and twenty simultaneous commands crashed the network.

SPOTLIGHT:
Behind the Tricky Details

"I didn't want people to be down on math," explains Naomi when she describes her presentations to the independent study seminar. "I love math, but I know sometimes people say, 'I'm not a math person' and tune you out." So, Naomi looked for real-world situations in which math saved the day, or at least explained why the day could not be saved. These were perfect, because her project, as well as her major in college, was applied mathematics.

Naomi's first presentation was tied to art forgery. Experts from many fields—art history, chemistry, and physics—had been trying to determine whether a painting was a genuine Vermeer or a fake. "The mathematicians figured it out," says Naomi with a bit of collegial pride. "They measured the rate of decay of uranium in the paint," she explains. "Differential equations were the key." Not that the equations were the key to Naomi's presentation style. "It didn't occur to me that my level of math would be different from my peers'. I thought integrals would be common knowledge, but only two people in the room knew what they were. People hadn't taken the same math courses I had." So Naomi quickly shifted from explaining what she calls "the tricky details" to the principle involved, "the idea behind the tricky details." Her classmates understood the steps she described, no equations required.

Naomi's work with her mentor, though, was all about the "tricky details." She solved problems from her mentor's college textbook during the first half of the year, and then moved on to numerical analysis, a topic he had not studied in depth. "He was still a guide," she says. "He had more experience solving problems, so he could grasp the concept before I could." It was a learning experience for both of them, Naomi believes, and her mentor now incorporates some of Naomi's work into the traditional classes he teaches.

Mathematics

One of my favorite math moments in independent study came via Ruthie, whose project comprised three topics, the first of which was chaos theory. To illustrate how small changes, over many iterations, add up to a huge difference, Ruthie started a game of "telephone," with students passing a message along via whisper. The opening phrase and the ending phrase had nothing in common, to the students' amusement. Ruthie was skilled not only at math but also at explaining math to students who knew less about the subject than she did. "People tend to get scared of formulas," she says. "If you can refer to something they are already familiar with as an example of the concept, you bring them into the math." Ruthie uses that skill now as a quantitative scientist working for a pharmaceutical company. A few math tips:

- *projects* Students have worked their way through math texts, with the help of their mentor, or they have mastered math-oriented software to solve problems or model math concepts. The mentor checks their work and suggests other solutions or methods. Chris Jones, math teacher and frequent mentor, described working with one extremely advanced student this way: "I was a sounding board. He'd come to our meeting and say, 'I did these problems. Here's one I like. Is there another way to do it?' Then he would walk me through his solution and I might suggest something he could try." Jones was not actively teaching the math; he was monitoring the student as the student taught himself.
- *product* To show what they have learned from a math project, students sometimes submit a problem set or a paper explaining or incorporating math principles. Some students have made computer programs to represent their work visually.
- *presentation* Math presentations can be tricky, as students in the class run the gamut from allergic-to-numbers to I-love-algorithms. Jones recommends that presenters make peace with the fact that some students will not grasp everything. "That's fine, so long as they grasp *something*," he says. In other words, think of the presentation as a buffet. Some will nibble, others will gobble, and most of the

class will have a light meal. Where possible, presenters should relate the mathematical concept to real-world phenomena.

SOCIAL STUDIES PROJECTS

I have never understood how history teachers cope with the fact that what they are supposed to teach grows every year, as current events become, well, history. And I am awed when I consider that, in addition to history, social studies comprises economics, geography, politics, sociology, and more. All aspects of social studies appear in independent study, as the projects in the sidebar illustrate.

Some words of advice about social studies projects:

• *projects* Most mentors encourage students to look for primary sources where possible; fortunately, digitized documents make this task easier. Since the COVID-19 pandemic began, more and more events have been posted on the web; lectures that once required in-person attendance can now be accessed online. Counsel your students to be wary, though. Some sites or speakers promote a particular point of view, and advocacy sometimes mars accuracy. Furthermore, because social studies is a broad designation, students may need help identifying subtopics and relevant search terms for their research. They may also need a bit of prodding to consider alternative points of view. An example: the conflict known as the "Vietnam War" in the United States is the "American War" to the Vietnamese. That small point reflects an important shift in perspective. Whether students opt for a broad or narrow set of sources, they should do so consciously. Also, not all sources are written. Interviewing living witnesses is a great way to expand skills and content. Remind students that record-keeping and proper citation are crucial, regardless of the type of source.

> third parties in US elections
> Sino-American relations
> climate change and economics
> post-Soviet Russia
> reunification of Germany
> American history through political cartoons
> the Yemeni conflict
> the Amarna period in ancient Egypt

- *products* A paper is the most common way of reporting information in this sort of project, but activism, videos, infographics, oral histories, timelines, maps, and statistical displays also work well and develop additional skills.

- *presentation* Social studies sometimes seems to be more accessible than it is; in discussion, students may chime in with "information" not based on fact but rather on common rumors. Prepare presenters for this sort of situation, and step in yourself if needed. One good tactic is to ask, "What is your source on that?" If there is none, the presenter can point out that the comment is speculative. If there is, the source can be evaluated. Visuals, too, should be sourced and checked for accuracy.

SPOTLIGHT:
Do They Learn This in Other Schools?

"We learn so much about World War II in our history classes, and we learn a lot about American history in general. But we learn almost nothing about my topic," says Garrett. "I wanted to know more." Garrett's topic was the internment of Japanese Americans from 1942 to 1945 in concentration camps, mostly in the western United States. In a heightened atmosphere of fear and anger after the bombing of Pearl Harbor, about 120,000 people of Japanese ancestry, more than sixty percent of them United States citizens, were forcibly relocated. "It's unique in American history," notes Garrett. "When I made my first presentation about it, the class was amazed. People said things like 'I knew nothing at all about this.' Some asked me, 'Do they learn this in other schools?' Mostly, they don't."

In addition to his research on the internment, Garrett read about Muslim Americans before and after the terrorist attacks of September 11, 2001. He compared their experiences with those of Japanese Americans during the war. Garrett notes wider parallels: "The internment is a way to see the experiences of other immigrants." He adds, "I'm Asian American myself, so I can empathize with what those families went through."

His independent study filled a gap in his education and also strengthened his research skills. "I know how important it is to be able to learn independently, especially in college. The independent study class was good preparation for that."

ARTS

Appreciation or studio work or both—an arts project nourishes the spirit and, as one student told me, "officially declares that my creativity matters." A sampling of arts projects appears below.

As this list reveals, independent study participants immerse themselves in the arts in a host of ways. Below are some recommendations for facilitating arts projects.

Performance and studio projects

• If a student is choreographing a ballet, who will dance it? Where will they practice? Who will chaperone? The main point here is to plan ahead and consider every detail, a resolution I made after a student pursuing a choreography project and I spent a year hauling desks to the wall so her dancers could jeté across the classroom. I had checked everything relating to the public performance and had completely forgotten about rehearsal. Music performance and theater projects also need designated space and storage, as may visual art projects.

• Another issue arises when self-expression conflicts with community norms. You want to encourage creativity, but also responsibility. Early on, perhaps in the proposal stage, discuss guidelines with the student. Agree on general principles. Require an "artist's statement" so students have to articulate their intentions and provide context.

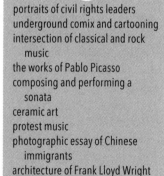

portraits of civil rights leaders
underground comix and cartooning
intersection of classical and rock music
the works of Pablo Picasso
composing and performing a sonata
ceramic art
protest music
photographic essay of Chinese immigrants
architecture of Frank Lloyd Wright and Zaha Hadid

- Grading a performance or studio project can be challenging unless you use a pass/fail system, in which case the fact that the performance took place or the painting exists is generally all you have to know. When finer distinctions must be made, decide beforehand what "counts." If the stage direction is good but the actors are not, does that affect the director's grade? What weight will you give to technique and what to the idea behind the sculpture? Arts teachers (and therefore arts mentors) are accustomed to making these decisions, though not all are accustomed to explaining their rationale. Try to go beyond "I know superior/inferior work when I see it." Ask mentors to write a critique, not just assign a grade.

- In the language arts section of this chapter, I discuss creative blocks in relation to writing projects. The same issues can occur in other creative projects. Jordan, looking back on his theater project, loved that "there wasn't a list of deliverables or a reading checklist" and that the important element was "the road and not the product at the end." Nevertheless, he understands that there must be accountability: "The surest way to not have something on the stage is not to schedule a first preview." He defines a deadline as "a scheduled opportunity," one that is necessary for creative work.

SPOTLIGHT:
Wow, I Accomplished This Thing

"I doodled all the time in English class," David told me. I already knew that, because it was *my* English class he was doodling in. I didn't mind, though, because David's doodles were classwork—just not for the class he was sitting in while he drew them, which was sports journalism. I was also David's independent study seminar leader, and his project was to write and draw a comic book. Doodles = drawings = work. Besides, I knew he could listen to the journalism class discuss an article while he was sketching and not miss a word.

"I drew all the time," David explained, "and I always loved comic books. With independent study, I could channel that energy into something productive. It was a source of pride to me that I could make a comic book." Entitled *Holy Moses*, David's comic book is a satirical look at high school, with special emphasis on the college admissions process. A few panels from *Holy Moses* appear at the beginning of this chapter. In another panel, not shown, a character yells at an obsessed applicant, "Ivy League this! Ivy League that! You talk about ivy so much you may as well go to horticulture college."

Buoyed by his independent study experience, David drew a daily comic strip in college. "I wouldn't have attempted that if I hadn't done my project. There was a 'wow, I accomplished this thing' feeling. That gave me confidence." Independent study also gave him a lesson in time management. Because he procrastinated, he had to pull more than one all-nighter to complete the work before my ultimate, no-matter-what-don't-be-later-than-this deadline. But he did complete the work, in fine fashion. His comic book is hilarious.

"When I proposed the project, I had not really thought about *how* to draw," David said. "My only thoughts were about the story. But my mentor [an art teacher] gave me books about cartooning, as well as books about how to tell a story through art. He would look at my work and suggest that I try different perspectives, things like that. I would draw the same image again and again, experimenting. He really pushed me artistically." David, in turn, pushed the seminar in an artistic direction. During his first presentation, he had students draw cartoon panels to tell their own stories. Later, he gave a lesson on perspective, showing how the artist can shift the reader's point of view to aerial, profile, and so forth.

David is not an artist now; he is a history teacher at the school he once attended. He often supervises independent study projects, guiding the next generation and, I imagine, doodling his way through mentor–student meetings.

Appreciation, history

- The same general parameters for research in any field apply to projects focusing on artistic movements, artists, or genres. Such work has been made easier as online art resources proliferated during pandemic closures. Some videos of performances or lectures require payment, but much is free. Remind students of possible bias in labeling. The "greatest" performance that pops up in an internet search has likely been chosen from a limited selection—what has been recorded and made available to the general public.
- The product of an art project lends itself to a multimedia format. Why write a paper about a musical work without including a link to the recording?
- Students preparing their products and presentations should know that reproducing an image for educational purposes is generally fine, but wide distribution beyond the school may not be. Students have to credit the artist(s) and be sure that what they are planning falls into the category of "fair use."

INTERDISCIPLINARY

Truth be told, more independent study projects than not are interdisciplinary. Knowledge in the real world does not sit in silos, so why should projects? In fact, I tend to encourage students to explore their topic through the lens of another discipline. A literature project might consider the psychological principles underlying a text, or the historical events that inspired it, or adaptations into different media or all of these aspects, as you see in the list of projects on the next page.

The subject-area tips earlier in this chapter apply to interdisciplinary work also, plus these:

- Consider co-mentors for interdisciplinary projects. A history teacher and a music teacher can tag-team a project on protest songs; a science teacher and an English teacher can guide a student's analysis of Margaret Atwood's *Oryx and Crake*, with one mentor discussing genetic engineering and the other literary style.

- Working with more than two mentors can be problematic. Who is meeting with whom when? The likelihood of three teachers and one kid answering that question the same way is not strong. For complicated projects, it is better to have one mentor, with occasional consultations on an ad hoc basis.

- Different disciplines have different citation formats. (Turf wars, I can't help thinking.) Before the project begins, the student and mentor(s) should decide which system makes the most sense.

the physics of time travel, time travel in literature and film
history and architecture of Liberia
science of *Star Trek*
mythology and poetry
the business of film
environmental racism
urban farming and the real estate industry
narrative in literature and film
the math and kinesiology of softball pitching
psychological disorders and criminal behavior portrayed on television
superheroes as a psychological reflection of the historical era in which they were created

SPOTLIGHT:
Spoke and Wheel

A well-defined question: that is the start, and the heart, of many independent study projects. But not all! Emily's project resembled a wheel, with her interest in global health ethics as the hub. Despite the fact that Emily formulated her independent study proposal in the spring of 2020, amid an exponentially rising number of COVID-19 cases, she did not limit her research to that disease. Instead, she approached her primary topic through a variety of subtopics, the spokes of the wheel. First, Emily took a historical approach, examining past clinical trials conducted on human subjects in developing countries. "I found aspects that came under ethical scrutiny," she explains. Her mentor, science teacher Lisa Rosenblum, says the goal for this portion of the project was to see how "concerns with those studies led to new protocols and new definitions of best practices." Next, Emily researched the global response to other pandemics, such as SARS (Severe Acute Respiratory Syndrome), Ebola, and Zika. She looked at media coverage, public perception, and allocation of health care resources. Only then did she turn to the pandemic she was living through, examining the transmission of disease from animals to humans, unequal access to health care, the role of the World Health Organization, political pressure, and other relevant factors. Though Emily followed many paths, they all led her to one destination—a better understanding of the complexity of global health ethics.

Unlike Emily, James began with the spokes and only gradually saw the hub. During our first conversation about independent study, his agile mind alighted on topic after topic. He was interested in everything and clearly capable of doing a great project on just about anything. As we talked, I made a private decision not to rein him in; this was a student who could and should explore. And so he did. His focus shifted radically during each of the year's three grading periods, from the game Connect Four to romance novels to fiction by Canadian writer Robertson Davies. When James analyzed the game, he used math to define patterns likely to lead to a successful outcome. As he worked his way through a shelf's worth of love stories, he noted patterns in the books and in fans' reactions, then deepened his understanding by consulting Janice A. Radway's *Reading the Romance: Women, Patriarchy, and Popular Literature.* In Davies's novels, James searched for stylistic and thematic links. James looks back at independent study and says, "I got a lot out of it. I loved the variety of the seminar, the eclectic mix of projects, the many different approaches and ideas. I never knew what to expect when I went in." But, he adds, "I don't think I had a coherent, year-long project." I disagree. The commonality—the hub—was pattern. That is what James really wanted to study. In some ways, it still is. A professor and writer specializing in intellectual property law and technology, James is currently writing a book that "explores the linguistic parallels between software and legal texts." In other words, pattern.

I gathered the suggestions in this chapter from a set of notebooks in which I kept track of projects and presentations through the years. They are filled with descriptions of success, the moments when a project or the student doing it surpassed all expectations. But there are warnings in my notebooks too, arising from situations in which things did *not* go to plan. If you are fortunate enough to direct an independent study group, you should keep a journal also. Consult it from time to time, to improve your own work and the chances that students, with your help, will improve theirs.

CHAPTER 6

Samuel's origami dragon. His independent study project was to build and program a machine to pre-crease the fold lines of origami shapes.

Independent Study as a Homeschooling Option

I ndependent study is all about (surprise!) independence, something homeschoolers declare when they decide that their children's educational journey will take place outside a traditional school setting. Two core elements of independent study—student-led projects and adult guidance—mesh seamlessly with homeschool practices. A third element, students teaching what they have learned, is achievable with a bit of ingenuity. In this chapter I explain how, and I show you ways to increase your students' independence *and* study.

THE PROJECT

Every aspect of school-based independent study projects I discuss in Chapter 2 is the same for homeschoolers, too, with one tiny difference: it is all easier. As a homeschooler, you have the advantage of observing your student all the time. Therefore, defining the project is simple. Your student may come to you: "I saw some ants in the kitchen. What do they eat? Why are you making that face?" And then they are off and running on a project about ant behavior and human behavior in response to ants. You can also start the conversation: "Yesterday you were playing chess with your cousin all afternoon. What do you like about the game?" The answer may be a shrug (kid-speak for "back off") or something like "figuring out a counterattack." That is an opening you should take advantage of: "Would you like to study chess strategy? Maybe check out some biographies of great chess players to understand their favorite moves?" These questions may lead to a study of the game (history, tactics, competitions) or perhaps research on child prodigies or gender issues in chess. In homeschooling, as in real life, interest may lead to inquiry and then to still more inquiry. Before you know it, a project is born. If you nudge the project along, remember that the ideas and approach must ultimately be the student's—a key difference from some other types of project-based learning.

I should point out that independent study doesn't have to dominate a homeschooling plan. A project can be the equivalent of a semester elective in a traditional curriculum, or one student-led unit in a group of units you select. Both bring a welcome change of pace as well as an invaluable benefit. Eric Chandler, head of the upper division at Kent Denver School, puts it this way: "Choosing a topic and saying 'this is what I want to study' gives you an academic identity as a person who can learn."

Mentoring independent study projects is also easier for homeschoolers. You set the household schedule, so finding common time to meet entails nothing more than entering "independent study" on the calendar. Because you can hand over teaching responsibilities, mentoring may also free up time in your day. Say you have a teenager or a middle schooler who will devote a semester to independent study:

Week 1: You want to learn about ants? Okay, go on the internet and find some articles and videos. Write a little bit about each source—where you found it, who created it, and when. [Student is working on ants; you are doing something else.]

Week 2: Still interested in ants? Okay, it is time for you to make a plan. Which sources are you going to use? How much will you read each week? What questions about ants do you want to answer? [Student is working on the proposal (see Chapter 2); you are doing something else. Then the two of you hammer out any issues until you are both satisfied.]

Next few weeks: Student researches ants. Once a week you check the notes and talk about ants.

Sometime later: "You have lots of notes about ants and pesticides. Are you interested in learning more about those chemicals?" [Student evaluates the direction of the project and adjusts as necessary, with your approval.]

See how it goes? You are not entirely free, but the responsibility, and the bulk of the work, shifts away from you. This is a bonus for homeschoolers who have a long to-do list, which is pretty much every homeschooler, ever. In addition to saving you time, independent study also empowers the student. We all want kids to learn responsibility, but they cannot do so unless they practice. A middle schooler generally needs higher guardrails around the project than a teenager, but you know your child better than anyone. Increase or decrease supervision based on your student's needs.

One note of warning: be wary of trying to extend a project beyond the child's interest. You want the student to make a commitment, but not one cast in titanium. Together with the student, decide on a reasonable amount of time for the project. For younger kids, shorter is probably better. Allow flexibility; if the project ignites curiosity, the time frame can expand. If there's less than meets the eye, let the student move on to something else.

A few more thoughts on projects in a homeschool setting:

- Your student should keep a work log (see Chapter 2), and you should do so also. When you inform government officials or college admissions officers that independent study has been one of your child's courses, you will need adult-generated records. (More on meeting educational standards appears later in this chapter.)

- Independent study is normally an individual endeavor, but home-schooled siblings can work together. Suppose your teenager wants to know more about ant colonies. To the web the teenager goes, in search of scientific papers. The middle schooler sets up an ant colony (or checks the kitchen cabinets!), and documents ant behavior. They can collaborate on some tasks, such as an experiment comparing ants' reaction to sweet, salty, and bitter food sources. The older child writes the lab report; the younger makes charts and illustrations.

- Creating a tangible expression of learning is also often easier in a homeschool setting, if the product is not a paper. (Writing a paper is the same no matter where students are.) If your student's product involves art or science materials, you do not have to justify your supply list to an administrator ("I need a model skeleton for this project. No, the Halloween decorations are not good enough."). Nor do you have to compete for display or storage space with other teachers. On the other hand, you do not have a school's budget supporting you. Check local schools and businesses to see whether any equipment may be borrowed or rented, and tap into your homeschool network for help. (No network? Keep reading to learn how to find and join one.)

- Your mentorship may be all the guidance your student needs, but do not be afraid to reach out to experts if the project lies beyond your comfort zone. If the student's research narrows the topic to a subtopic and then narrows again to a subtopic of a subtopic (in other words, into minutiae), a consultant can be a great help. Someone who really knows the subject can put together a reading list or suggest avenues of research. Check with your homeschooling network or call a university in your area. There may be a graduate student who is desperate to talk about that sub-sub-subtopic. Check online for groups that share your student's interest: stamp collecting, Jane Austen, the Revolutionary War, whatever. (Other suggestions for mentor-hunting appear in Chapter 2.) Once you have found someone, triple check and monitor interactions between your student and anyone you do not know well. "Stranger danger" is rare but real.

One last word on projects: you can buy books or card sets with step-by-step explanations of hundreds of projects. Created by experienced teachers, these are great resources. They are *not* independent study projects, as I define the term, because the teacher, not the student, has designed the work.

THE SEMINAR

In Chapter 3, I discuss running a seminar in a traditional school context. Homeschoolers can form a seminar also. In fact, you may already have one. "You put the kids around the table and tell them that Seymour has spent a year studying rocks, and now he's going to teach what he's learned to you," says Jennifer Kaufeld, imagining independent study in a homeschool setting when there is more than one child in the group. A veteran homeschooler herself and the author of *Homeschooling for Dummies*, Kaufeld says that "independent study absolutely works" as part of a homeschooler's pedagogical tool kit.

But what if there is no sibling old enough to understand the subject? Parents can step in. Kaufeld describes a project one of her children came up with, exploring world geography through food. "He loves learning geography this way," she says. "He disappears and reads. He makes maps, and he figures out how the geographical features of a region relate to traditional foods. He asks questions: Why do they grow corn there? What dishes do they make with corn? Then he comes back and teaches it all to his parents." It is a small seminar, to be sure, but it is still a venue in which the student can function as a teacher.

Homeschoolers have other options for seminar, too. If you are part of a homeschooling co-op, ask whether members are interested in offering an independent study option. Tap into a homeschooling network in your area, recruiting students who are interested in pursuing an independent study. To find a network, check social media for groups in your area by entering your location and "homeschooling." You can also inquire about local networks by contacting the homeschooling association of your state or province. You do not have to limit yourself to established networks. Talk with parents in the park, at the recreation center, or in your place of worship. Find out who is homeschooling, and ask whether they are interested in pursuing independent study. Search the internet for homes-chooling blogs and post a query there, or hang a flyer in a store or library.

Once you have a group, or even just one partner, you have made inde-pendent study a part of your homeschooling curriculum. Parents assume the mentor role for their children, unless all agree to swap kids (just academically!). The group can get together, in person or virtually, for a half hour or so each week or for a longer stretch every few weeks. Adjust the timing to suit the age level and number of students in the group. As in a brick-and-mortar setting, the independent researchers take turns teaching their peers. They email homework to each other or post it on a website that they and their teachers can access. Homeschooling parents take turns supervising the seminar and evaluating the presenter's perfor-mance. When no presentation is scheduled, students use seminar time to share research tips or to describe the product they are working on. Student filmmakers can recommend the best apps to their classmates, and paper writers can describe how they arrived at a thesis. An adult may facilitate these conversations, so long as the focus remains on what students have to offer.

SPOTLIGHT:
Game Theory, Independently

When Laurie Block Spigel's younger son was seven, he was passionately interested in whales. Games, not so much. But his older brother had made countless fantasy games, so he decided to make one as well, with whales as its focus. The result-ing board game was simple but, with the freedom homeschool-ing granted him, he returned to the project two more times. The third and final version, which he made when he was twelve, is entitled "Whale Race." The game board is a world map with paths tracing the migratory routes of four different whales. Play-ers move forward by answering questions about these marine mammals.

Inspired by the combination of joy and education she saw in Whale Race, Spigel created a course in board game design that she offers to other homeschooled children, ages seven and up. Students in her class have an age-appropriate degree of independence: they select topics that intrigue them and do their own research. Spigel, who runs the resource-filled website homeschoolnyc.com, encourages her students to consult a variety of written and electronic sources and, if appropriate, to interview experts and visit museums and libraries.

The games students create express what they have learned about their topics, which have included global warming, ancient Greece, horses, the Frick Museum, orchids of Puerto Rico, chocolate, and many others. During class, students "brainstorm questions to jump-start the research process, which is question-based the way all good research is," explains Spigel. "They try to stump the class with newfound facts," an activity that places them in a teaching role, and they also refine their games with, Spigel notes, "new and sometimes daring designs appearing in every class."

The course culminates in "Game Day," during which students play the games they and their classmates created. "Parents have told me that they had to pull their child away from the computer at eleven p.m. so they would stop taking notes or writing fact cards for their games," Spigel says, noting that homework usually has the opposite effect. Industrious enthusiasm is evident in her "Make Your Own Board Game" course, a model any homeschooler can adopt.

REPORTING TO THE AUTHORITIES

Who tells homeschoolers what they have to do? The government (state or provincial, in the form of a board of education or a similar body), your local school district, and scariest of all—college admissions officers. Okay, that last bunch does not actually tell anyone what to do, but if you cannot show them that your homeschooled applicant has met or exceeded standards, your kid's application may end up, as Jennifer Kaufeld says, "in the pile labeled 'look at later if time permits.'" No one wants to be in that pile! Fortunately, it is easy to meet the expectations of all these authorities.

Government

If you have been homeschooling for a while, you are probably well versed in the requirements of your state or province, as well as those of your school district. (If not, the homeschooling association of your state or province can guide you.) An independent study project is no different from any other unit of learning you assign. The record-keeping system I describe in Chapter 2 is a good place to start. Students note the sources they consulted: title, author, date, publisher, and, for digital sources, the web address and date accessed. They list the papers they have written, the experiments they have done, and the products they have created. All that is for your benefit, and for the benefit of the student, who learns good work habits.

Once you have the student's records in hand, your job is to put the information into whatever format the authorities require. That format differs depending upon where you live. In general, all homeschoolers must create a transcript; many must compile a portfolio of work also.

A transcript is a list, a skeletal outline of what the student has done. It includes the course title ("independent study"), the academic year, the course grade, and the number of credits. Credit systems differ, but most award one credit for a year-long course, a half credit for a semester, and smaller fractions for shorter time frames. If your student's independent study is one unit out of many in a course, do not list it separately on the transcript.

A portfolio contains a sampling of student work. For independent study, tuck in papers, drawings, source lists, as well as photos of anything that is too large for a file folder or has more than two dimensions—performances, artwork, experiments, and so forth. The photos should document the process as well as the end result. Portfolios do *not* include everything the student has done. You're sending this to a teacher/administrator who is as overburdened as you are. Excerpts are sufficient unless you are told otherwise. The goal is to give a sense of the quality and quantity work the student did, and what the student learned in terms of skills and content.

Creating a transcript or portfolio is a pain, I know. Maybe this will help you feel better: Jennifer Kaufeld, homeschooling expert, points out that a single independent study project may tick several boxes on a list of required courses. Suppose your child is obsessed with ships and has spent a semester reading about them. Depending on what the student has done, the project may count as

- *art* design, decoration
- *mathematics* calculation of how fast, how far, how often the ship travels
- *history* movement of goods, dominance of sea routes
- *science* environmental impact, physics of water travel

Because independent study projects tend to be interdisciplinary, the credits they earn are flexible, and you can use them to plug a gap in the transcript. This may sound slightly shady, but it is not. The student is working very hard. Putting that work into boxes is the questionable activity, in my view, not truthfully explaining the subjects the project relates to. Just be honest about time. If you count the project as a full-year course, the student should work approximately 120 hours on it. That is not a lot: a forty-week school year is the norm, so you are talking about three hours a week. When you count seminar meetings, work time, and mentor meetings, independent study work can easily exceed that number.

On beyond high school

Your homeschooled student's high school education is almost complete. Congratulations to both of you! In an ideal world you would have a moment to rest on your laurels, but in the world we actually inhabit, it is time to plan for the next step: perhaps a job, the military, vocational training, or college. While students reflect on their future, homeschoolers must prepare documentation to show that their students are indeed well educated. Every student needs a transcript (see above), but the label "independent study" covers a wide range of work. In a traditional school setting, administrators prepare a curriculum booklet that describes their course offerings. The booklet goes to admissions officers and to any others who need to know what the student has studied. In a homeschool setting, the task of describing the curriculum falls to you.

A description of independent study as it played out in your home should include the following:

- *project* Identify the topic, state the frequency of mentor meetings, and the sources consulted. If the source list is long, cite a couple and label them "representative."
- *mentor* Include this information only if someone with specialized knowledge worked with the student (a professional musician, a nutritionist, a weaver, and so forth).
- *product* Give the type and size ("two five-page papers," "six ceramic pieces," "one 45-minute piano recital," and the like).
- *seminar* Explain how often the group met and what was accomplished during meetings.

For more detail on describing independent study to admissions officers and hiring managers, see Chapter 8. I also discuss student-written admissions essays in that chapter.

You embarked on homeschooling so that you could have a say in your children's education. With independent study, you cede some power to your students. When you do so, they will feel, as I know you do, the satisfaction that comes from meaningful work.

CHAPTER 7

Dorin's photo of a pair of high heels, one image from
a portfolio she created as an independent project for her
photography class.

Independent Study Units
Within a Traditional Class

t was February, a cruel month in my climate. My eleventh-grade
English students were in the final stage of my go-to assignment for a
drab, winter week: select a poem, analyze its form and content, and report
to the group. The class was quiet (they were well-behaved kids), but I
doubt many were really listening to the presenter's insights on "Mending
Wall." More than a few pairs of eyes had glazed over, and no one but me
was taking notes. I sighed and wondered why I was not seeing the energy
of the independent study seminar I had attended a few hours earlier. Was
there a way to capture that magic and pour it into a traditional class?

Yes, there was a way—in fact, several ways. It took me a while to find
them, but eventually I learned how to apply independent study techniques

to "regular" lessons. So have my colleagues in other disciplines, some inspired by watching presentations on subjects outside their own field of expertise. Jennifer Little, an English teacher and seminar leader, recalls a student's work on "high level physics concepts—relativity, quantum mechanics, string theory. He was so amazingly good at presenting complicated concepts that I learned something about teaching from him. He could bring a concept alive. What a lovely quality to appreciate in one of your students!"

In this chapter I explain how to apply independent study techniques to traditional coursework and give you a close look at these techniques in action in a few classes. I hope you will be inspired to consciously experiment with independent work, either as an altogether new approach or as a small adjustment to an assignment or strategy you are already using.

DIFFERENT SETTING, SAME PRINCIPLES

The essentials of independent study are few: the student leads, the adult guides, and students teach their peers. This sounds simple, but questions arise. If students are leading, is the curriculum still valid? Is it possible for teachers to adopt a mentoring role while conducting a class? Can students actually teach? The answers: yes, yes, and yes.

Student leadership

Teachers of required courses are constrained by a prescribed curriculum, unlike those directing independent study, which has no curriculum except what students have fashioned by and for themselves. With some inventiveness, though, any teacher can place students in a leadership role.

What do you want to know? We do not often ask kids that question. As educators, we assume that *we* know what they should know, and often that assumption is correct. Yet students remain curious. If we want them to see themselves as learners throughout their lives, we need to validate their curiosity. Some ways to do so:

- Put a "wonder box" in the classroom or create a "wonder file" on the class website. Encourage students to pose questions relating to the unit the class is studying: "I wonder whether there are any endangered species around here." "What is the largest prime number?" "Is the Electoral College good or bad for democracy?" "Can music change people's point of view?"

- At set intervals—once a week, perhaps—the students select questions they would like to answer. Working individually or in small groups, they research their own or someone else's question or participate in activities (observing nature, for instance, or listening to protest songs).

- Schedule class time for the sharing of results—every other Friday, for instance. Permit a question to carry over to subsequent weeks if it remains unanswered.

- Don't let this assignment overburden students. If they cannot finish during class, reduce other homework. Adding to their workload punishes curiosity.

- Human nature being what it is, someone may drop an inappropriate question into the wonder box or come up with wrong or rude answers. Vet everything students submit, extract anything offensive before others see it, and have a serious talk with writers who have strayed out of bounds.

My plan is . . . This variation of "what do you want to know?" involves students committing to a long-term project of their own design, within your class, working in a way that makes sense for them.

- Recast the prompts or parameters of an existing assignment, ceding some control to the students. Say you generally supply a list of research topics. Set it aside and instead explain the criteria the list is based on. Permit students to search out something that meets your standards. An example: I used to name a dozen or so Harlem Renaissance works we had not read as a group and ask each student to choose one. My list was intended to deepen students' understanding of the themes and issues that preoccupied the artists of that era. At some point I withdrew the list and asked students to "select a work created during the Harlem Renaissance and relate it to the themes and issues of the era." Some students found writers new to me; others pushed the boundaries past literature, with my blessing: an Aaron Douglas painting, a Jelly Roll Morton jazz song, and newspaper articles from *The Crisis*, a publication of the National Association for the Advancement of Colored People (NAACP), one of the most prominent civil rights organizations of the era. As they shared their work with each other, I realized that the results were far richer than those I had received in prior years.

• For selected assignments, encourage students to experiment with different ways of expressing what they have learned: by building an interactive website, giving a performance, circulating a petition to elected officials, creating an artwork, starting a podcast, and so forth.

• Let them regulate the timing, within limits. For example, ask each student to propose a customized schedule for submitting the stages of a research paper: source list, notes, outline, rough draft, and final draft. Specify the parameters for every step ("during the first two weeks of November," "before winter break"). Bonus: instead of swamping you, work trickles in, and your daily to-do list feels a lot more manageable.

Opt out. An opt-out assignment presents the lesser of two evils or, for the enthusiastic, the greater of two joys. Give your usual assignment and provide an alternate. Test on Friday? Students can write a paper if they prefer. Quiz tomorrow? Write a journal entry instead. Here is an especially creative example from a school near New York's Metropolitan Museum of Art: an English teacher assigned an essay in response to a poem. When the class groaned, he offered another option. Before the end of the following week, they could visit the Met and snap a photo of a painting expressing the same themes as the poem, justifying their selection in written form or in an audio recording. About half the class made the museum trip; most who did so took the audio option. Their insights into the poem were as good if not better than the level of analysis in the essays. They also learned something about art and, as an added benefit, developed public-speaking skills. Some even became dedicated museumgoers!

Adult guidance

I have attended more than one lecture on pedagogy in which the speaker implied that to be "the sage on the stage" was hopelessly old-fashioned, almost an educational felony. This was always conveyed without a trace of irony, despite the fact that the lecturer was generally on a stage while espousing the wisdom of being "a guide on the side." Most educators I know are quite comfortable on the side. I like it there myself and, in the independent study course, I take that role to the extreme. In a traditional class I push it, but not as far. (For a great model of a "guide on the side," see "A Closer Look at Three Independent Study Units" later in this chapter.)

Questioning questions. Teachers tend to be explainers (I know I am), so it is hard not to answer kids' questions. But probing can be more effective than laying everything out. Here is a fabricated but realistic interchange:

> **Student:** Why do we add white vinegar to this solution instead of cider vinegar?
> **Teacher:** What could be a reason?
> **Student:** Maybe white vinegar is different.
> **Teacher:** In what way?
> **Student:** Well, they are different colors. And they taste different, too. Maybe there is something in cider vinegar that is not in white vinegar.
> **Teacher:** Would you like to look it up?

The student hits the internet and finds out that white vinegar averages 2.5 pH, compared to cider vinegar's 3.5 pH. That information leads to a conversation about what determines pH levels and why cider vinegar is more acidic. This sort of learning takes more time than a statement from the teacher, because discovering always proceeds more slowly than covering. However, the knowledge gained tends to be more meaningful to the student.

The mentor will see you now. Suppose students are working on individual projects with a common theme. You do not have time to see each student during a free period. Hence, mentoring must take place during class. You can (and probably already do) roam around the room, stopping here and there to read over their shoulders while students work. Make things a bit more formal by scheduling appointments. Set aside a period, or two for a larger group, during which students work independently. Post a schedule of five-minute slots, and ask students to sign up for one. At the allotted time, they meet you in your "office"—your desk or a virtual breakout room—to discuss their progress. Because the meetings are short, train them to be succinct (an important life skill). Needless to say, during each appointment scan the room with your teacher radar set to maximum, so you can forestall potential trouble.

Inviting visitors. Lots of independent study programs work with outside mentors (see Chapters 2 and 4 for examples), so why not your class? It may not be possible for mentors to visit your room, but students can meet with their mentors online or via phone. Tap into the school and community network to find learning partners for specific projects, and vet mentors carefully. Monitor student–mentor interactions by requiring students to record online meetings or calls, and mandate that students log their work so you can keep track of their progress. (See Chapter 2 for more about work logs for independent projects.)

Evaluation. You cannot stay on the sidelines for this one, because grades are your responsibility. However, you may want to ask the students to reflect on their projects and to submit a written statement about what they believe went well and what they would do differently the next time. Have them address process as well as progress. Press for details, and distribute a form tailored to suit the project. Appendix B provides a sample form that might be used for a history research project.

Students Teaching Peers

Aristotle viewed teaching as the highest form of understanding. Perhaps that is why many schools have tutoring programs, within the school or in the larger community. With well-designed assignments, this extracurricular activity can also be curricular.

Designated content specialists. Students, either individually or in a small group, can research a topic that interests them. When they learn enough, they become "designated specialists" who offer information and insights to their classmates. Say an American history class is studying the 1920s. Let students choose an area to focus on—the stock market, women's suffrage, the League of Nations, the Great Migration, Prohibition, and so forth. During class discussion, specialists weigh in when their information is relevant. In language arts, students may choose a character, theme, or plot point from the literary work the class is reading. The designated specialists pay close attention to the aspect of the work they selected. During discussions of F. Scott Fitzgerald's *The Great Gatsby*, for example, the "Nick Carraway specialist" may chime in with an analysis of Nick's evolving view of the title character. The "American Dream specialist" can offer insight into Gatsby's quest to change his identity. You remain quiet while the specialists speak, interrupting only to correct errors or redirect the discussion.

Skill specialists. "Skill specialists" earn that title by demonstrating mastery. In a science class, you may have a "slide specialist" who expertly prepares specimens for examination under a microscope or a "spreadsheet specialist" who knows how to organize data. During class, other students turn to these specialists when they need assistance. (Chapter 4 describes how middle school science teachers at Seattle Country Day School employ this approach.) For a writing assignment in any subject, you can also slot in problem-solving time, during which specialists in thesis-statement formation, revision, and punctuation assist their peers.

Teaching, not reporting. At the beginning of this chapter I described a junior English class mired in the February doldrums, with each student dutifully reporting on a poem. I liked the "choose your own literary work" aspect of the assignment, as well as the chance to strengthen students' public-speaking skills. But the reports were boring. Fortunately, the solution was simple. I made every reporter into a teacher, à la independent study, and told the class I would evaluate whatever the presenter said *and* everything the class contributed. Eureka! Kids got more involved, because when it was their turn, they knew they would benefit from what their peers added to the discussion. When they got more involved, they perked up. So did I.

Here are a few details about my poetry assignment. The plan adapts easily to anything students can discuss in one class period, be it literature or not:

- When I start the unit, I teach a few poems myself so they have a model.
- I define the set they choose from: sonnets, contemporary poets, war poetry, and the like.
- If the class is large, I form groups of three or four and tell them they are co-teaching the poem. I suggest that teams assign areas of focus to each member (the "designated specialists" I describe earlier in this chapter).
- I pass along a few teaching tips (see Chapter 3) and offer help but not answers as they prepare.
- I do not subtract points if someone in the class makes an error or if the presenter cannot answer a question, unless it relates to something the presenter should know.
- The "teachers" can call on students. They may also offer an activity, if I have preapproved it.

I handle any students who stray off task. I want students to be teachers, but the disciplinary role and responsibility for the class remain with me.

SUBJECT-AREA COURSES AND INDEPENDENT STUDY

I took many science courses when I was a student. I was mildly interested in all of them, but only one remains in my memory. On the first day of twelfth grade, our physics teacher announced that we would not be learning physics from him. Instead, we would be designing and conducting experiments and deducing the principles of physics from our results. Anything in the storage closet was fair game, and he would be available if things went awry. He would offer tips if we were really floundering, but basically the responsibility for learning was ours. The challenges he posed were sometimes broad ("figure out what affects momentum"), sometimes specific ("build a scale that can weigh a feather"). My favorite was "redesign this model car so it runs faster." We worked in groups of three, and although at least two hours a week had been blocked off for physics lab work, my group devoted many lunch hours and evenings to experimenting on that vehicle. On its final run, the toy sped off before we could catch it and sailed right through a window. A *closed* window. We had to pay for a replacement pane of glass, but none of us minded. We had built a fast car. Even better, we knew why it was fast.

That was a course specifically designed to empower students. It was a science elective, but the principles adapt to other disciplines as well. Social studies, for example: in Chapter 4, I describe Urban Academy's "Choose Your Own Adventure" class. Math, too: one teacher, Chris Jones, concludes an advanced course with a capstone project. For a few weeks, students work individually or with one partner. "The projects are something they are super-interested in," Jones explains, and the topics vary widely. When the work is completed, each student or pair has one full period to teach the class. "It's a mini independent study," Jones says. "I like to end the year with the kids actively engaged. Also, when they are forced to explain something to someone else, they understand it more, and they know that they are a member of a learning community." Jones's approach can work with less advanced students, too. In a middle school math class, for example, the teacher can ask students to dig more deeply into a topic they studied. They can look at several textbooks to see how each explains, for instance, "least common denominator." Then they can formulate their own explanations and teach or review the concept with the class—an excellent year-end assignment.

The "mini independent study" model can also be adapted to a language class. Students can search out new words or phrases pertaining to an event or location, practice the pronunciation with your help, and then devise a way to teach the vocabulary to their classmates. Students can also research cultural traditions and prepare a lesson about them.

One student of Japanese became intrigued by kamishibai, a traditional form of storytelling via a series of drawings. She repurposed a cardboard box and attached a frame. Then she slotted in drawings, one at a time, to illustrate the story she was reciting to her classmates. Note: if students' accents are acceptable, they can handle the entire lesson. If not, they can give you their lesson plans and have you read the script.

A CLOSER LOOK AT THREE
INDEPENDENT STUDY UNITS

In relation to traditional pedagogy, independent study is an alternate universe. This section is a tour of that universe, with stops at a high school biology lab, a middle school science classroom, and a photography studio serving both age groups.

High School Biology

How does a fruit fly court a potential mate?
Does changing the air temperature, the age of the yeast, or the amount of sugar affect rising bread dough?
Do flatworms tend to move toward or away from light?

Students posed these questions and others in a year-long course, Experimental Biology, which Janet Kraus taught at the Horace Mann School for several years. All her students had already taken a standard survey class in biology, with teacher-planned lab sessions. Now they would design their own experiments based on three life-forms: yeast, fruit flies, and planaria (flatworms), each the subject of a ten-week unit. Before they could plan an experiment, though, they needed information. They could have done their own research on the internet and learned a few basic facts, but a deeper understanding would yield a better experiment. Plus, the point of the course was lab work.

That is where Kraus came in. In "sage mode," she introduced each unit with two weeks' worth of information about the organism the class was focusing on. After that, she turned into "the guide on the side" as students thrashed out experimental designs. Her comments pushed them to think like scientists. What had they observed? What question would their experiment attempt to answer? How would they gather data? How would they make a hypothesis and test it, then record and evaluate the results? Kraus says, "I was an ally, not a critic, in my approach. I knew they could do really fine projects." Occasionally, she had to step in with a reality check, explaining to one student that an experiment involving successive generations of fruit flies wasn't possible in ten weeks. The student moved to fruit fly behavior, placing one male and one female fly inside a glass beaker, timing and analyzing their movements. He repeated the procedure with two other varieties of fruit flies and compared the results.

All research took place during class; students kept daily journals of their work and presented the results to their peers and invited guests at the end of each unit. The course extended students' skills beyond science. They recorded data in a spreadsheet program, documented their work with photos or videos, and communicated information through a presentation app. Students also learned to place their work in context by surveying the literature, reading about other experiments with a similar focus. "The course showed them the route that professional scientists follow, including required peer review. They learned what it is like to actually do science," says Kraus—their sage and guide.

Middle School Science

Gaining independence is a gradual process, one that can begin early in students' academic journey. A good example is the middle school science curriculum at Metro Detroit's University Liggett School. As Andrea Champagne, a science teacher, explains, "In sixth grade they do a science project of their own choosing. They plan while they are in class and then work on the project at home or after school." Some may use the school's innovation lab, which is stocked with tools and computers. When the projects are complete, the students present their work during class. In seventh grade, students conduct an experiment and write a lab report, "scaling up their independence a little further." Champagne explains that during the following year, "they really dive in. We teach them how to come up with an idea and turn it into a question, and we show them how to find and evaluate sources." The students' next task is to formulate an experiment that will answer the questions they devised. If their question calls for such work, students use the innovation lab to engineer a design and test it. Whatever they do, teachers "show them how to analyze their data and put it in a lab report," says Champagne.

The project is the sole focus of the eighth-grade science class after spring break, a full quarter of the academic year. They work independently, but with strict guidelines: "There are checkpoints, deadlines when they have to complete each step, and rubrics to fill out: have you done this or not?" At regular intervals the teacher meets with each student individually during class and also assigns students to small groups. According to Champagne, "Team members help each other. They share how their project is going. Sometimes they say, 'I'm stuck, I don't know what to do' and the team is there to help. They act as a sounding board and offer ideas." Students display their final projects at a year-end "Celebration of Science," for which the students dress in business attire, a visual indication of the importance of the independent work they have done.

Photography

What do you want us to take pictures of?
What do *you* want to see?

Karen Johnson, a photographer and teacher of the art, explains that every year students in her beginners class ask the first question, which she answers by posing the second. The shift in power goes to the heart of her pedagogy. Johnson knows that she is the expert charged with explaining equipment and technique and stimulating awareness of the many different ways that photography is used artistically; she also knows that to be artists, students must explore their own vision. "I want to lead them to self-expression and away from 'this is what the teacher wants me to do.' They often come in with narrow assumptions about what a good photo is," she explains. "Most only consider the documentary potential of the image. Basically, they think 'there's my grandmother and here's a photo of my grandmother,' and if they can see her, it's a good picture."

It can be a multiyear process, with students' independence increasing gradually. Early on, Johnson gives an assignment she calls "Three Subjects." Students choose a realistic subject, an abstract subject, and one that is "symbolic or poetic." Johnson says the point is "to trigger the mind to think beyond what is there." Advanced students have still more freedom, and of course, more responsibility. They compile a portfolio each term or continue work on one they started previously. (The photo at the beginning of this chapter comes from one student's portfolio.) The assignment begins with a written proposal that states what they will do ("I will take a hundred digital photos" or "I will shoot six rolls of film") and, most important, what organizing principle or theme is at work ("photos depicting isolation" or "friends in poses paired with childhood photos" or "hand-colored photos of architectural subjects"). They must state how they will determine whether they have reached their goal for the project and must also keep a "source book." The source book includes other photographers' images, poetry, or other writings that have influenced the student's work, along with the student's commentary. Johnson writes questions and suggestions in the source books, which evolve into a mentor–student conversation. When the portfolios are complete, students present their work without an initial explanation and listen to classmates' critiques. Other students share what they are seeing and what it means to them. They also ask questions like "how did you get that effect?" Johnson joins in, but only after the students have had their turn. The final step is self-evaluation. The responsibility to assign a grade belongs to Johnson, who considers technical prowess and, most important, evidence of a developing, unique vision.

I doubt that you wish to clone any course—or even any assignment—described in this chapter. Your teaching style and the students you work with are unique, and therefore your classes are too. Instead of replication, take an idea you find interesting and change it. Make it your own! Keep track of successes and build on them. When a lesson falls flat, take notes and make adjustments. In other words, conduct your own independent study of independent study techniques.

CHAPTER 8

Jordyn's project gave rise to a lifelong interest in photography.
Shown here is his photo of driftwood on a Hawai'i beach.

Beyond the Classroom

I have always felt that directing independent study is the most fun job in a school. You get to be with kids and mentors who are excited about their work, and you get to learn a variety of things—*new* things— every year. But like any job, running an independent study program comes with responsibilities. Those pertaining to the project and seminar I describe at length in other chapters of this book. Here I move outside the classroom and discuss dealing with school administrators, parents, college admissions officers, and your students' potential employers. I also give you a glimpse of some independent study participants who have left their classroom years behind and gone on to fulfilling careers and lives, enriched by their experience in the program.

IS THIS A REAL COURSE?

I've heard that question spoken aloud only once or twice, but I've seen it much more often, written on polite faces. I understand the skepticism, because the label "independent study" has been pasted on a wide range of classes. Some are spectacular, and a few, spectacular failures. I believe that the program I advocate falls into the first category, but I also know that anyone involved with independent study has to answer the question over and over again, with transparency and a nod to public relations. To properly evaluate independent study, people need to see what the kids are doing. Some suggestions for taking the message beyond the classroom:

- *Open seminar presentations to guests.* Publish the schedule on the school website or in the faculty bulletin, well in advance, and issue an open invitation. Offer live streaming or asynchronous recordings to those who cannot attend in person.
- *Have students give presentations to other classes.* Speak with colleagues who teach courses related to the subject matter of an independent study project. They may welcome a guest teacher.
- *Schedule schoolwide presentations.* Check with the person responsible for school assemblies to see whether there is room for a couple of mini-presentations, each perhaps five to ten minutes long.
- *Expand to evenings and weekends.* Projects involving a capstone performance may acquire a larger audience if they are scheduled during nonschool time. Ditto for art exhibits.
- *Host an independent study festival.* University Liggett School in Michigan calls this year-end event a "Celebration of Research." Green Farms Academy in Connecticut frees students from classes for a "symposium," a day of workshops and presentations. St. Luke's, also in Connecticut, hosts an evening "Scholars Symposium" every April. The goal of all these events is the same: to showcase independent work.
- *Seek out those likely to share the same interests.* Invite the school band or glee club to a musical performance, the theater club to a play, drawing and painting classes to an art opening, and so forth.

- **Publish.** Poetry, short stories, and excerpts from longer works (novels, research papers, screenplays, etc.) may find a home in an existing school publication, or you can publish them yourself in an independent study magazine.
- **Send links.** If the class has a website, publicize the link, after password-protecting any pages that are restricted to participants only.
- **Contact school and local media.** Ask the school newspaper and alumni magazine to run articles about the course or individual projects; inquire whether local papers will send a reporter to cover a presentation or a capstone event. Post information about the course and the projects on social media (submitted through the school's account, with proper protection of student privacy).

All these initiatives depend upon your students' doing quality work—and upon your honesty, because some students do *not* produce quality work. You cannot and should not hide that fact. Kids are kids. A couple will lose interest or prioritize what even they see as "real classes" and consequently receive a low or failing grade in independent study. But the shortcomings of a few do not define the course. As Eric Chandler of the Kent Denver School puts it, "When students are given the opportunity to pursue projects of their own, there will be a couple who lowball it, but that doesn't mean the program itself is a failure. Furthermore, the student can learn from a missed opportunity." I agree with Dr. Chandler and add that every year, in every single one of my traditional classes, at least one student has underperformed, and no one has ever asked me whether English is a real class. We should not expect less of independent study students, but we should not expect more, either—even though we often get exactly that! Donavan, a former independent study participant, says that he invested "exponentially" more effort into his project, because he loved what he was doing. Josh says, "I don't remember my project being a huge time commitment. It was something I wanted to do, and I remember it as fun."

PARENT–CHILD BOUNDARIES

Another beyond-the-classroom issue with independent study is parental "help." I place that word in quotation marks because all educators have occasionally heard a parent say something like "we have a history project this weekend." Worse, all educators have encountered some parents who are so anxious about their child's performance that they sideline a student's imperfect effort and replace it with their own, more polished product. These issues can occur in any course, but independent study has no tests or quizzes. Hence the issue of adult interference may take on outsized importance. If this issue arises, encourage appropriate behavior in a number of ways:

- *Educate parents.* Every day in the classroom, teachers navigate the boundary between helping and usurping students' work. We know when to step forward and when to step back. Parents may not, so we have to explain: "It is fine to suggest sources, but students strengthen their research skills if they locate some books or websites themselves." "If your child needs a third hand when building something, offer yours, but please do not work on the project by yourself." "Suggestions are great; orders are not."
- *Check students' work and question any gaps.* Do not assume wrongdoing, but do ask: "I see notes on ten articles here. How did you get work done while you were on the community service trip?" If the answer is something like "my dad had a couple of days off that week," it is time for you, the student, and Dad to have a conversation.
- *Require a source list.* In their work logs, students must identify sources they consulted. Remind them that an adult's comment is, in fact, a source and must be cited. Keeping track is sometimes enough to forestall problems.

I would rather not end this section on a negative note, because collaboration between generations can be the best part of independent study. Rejoice in that, while encouraging respect for parent–child boundaries. Everyone involved will benefit.

COLLEGE AND OTHER ADMISSIONS

Scholarly journal articles or Wikipedia entries? Dozens of drawings leading to an oil painting or a few desultory sketches? Admissions officers from post-secondary schools (colleges, conservatories, vocational schools) cannot tell what went into a student's project and the seminar from a single transcript line reading "independent study." Therefore, someone—either the independent study director, another administrator, or the students themselves—must let them know. There are several ways to get this information into the right hands.

Course description

The school's list of required and elective courses informs students and parents about the school's offerings. Admissions officers may also see this document, either because the school has sent it or because they have sought the information online. The course description of independent study should be brief but specific. A sample description:

Independent Study Seminar

Full year, one credit, eight meetings per ten-day cycle

Prerequisites: open to eleventh or twelfth graders only, written application and interview required

The Independent Study Seminar allows motivated, responsible students to study topics not included in the curriculum or to continue research on a topic covered in a previous course. Students may also opt to pursue creative projects (writing a novel, composing music, painting, and so forth). Each student works independently, guided by a faculty mentor. Students meet with their mentors at least once per week and with the seminar director once every other week. Participants also gather in seminar five times per ten-day cycle. Students must log their work and create a product each trimester (usually a research paper, a literary or artistic work, a scientific experiment, a technical device,

> or a performance). During seminar sessions, students teach each other, drawing from the knowledge acquired through their independent work.

As you see, in just a few lines the description specifies the number of group and individual meetings, the degree of supervision, and the course requirements.

Project description

A course description is essential, but generic. In addition to information about the course, admissions officers should know exactly what the student's project involves. High school counselors can explain this in their recommendation letters, ideally providing a succinct but vivid explanation of the work and the student's commitment to it. Because the best descriptions are those that are well informed, it is a good idea for students to personally invite their counselors to presentations. Kaitlin Howrigan, a college counselor, makes a point of attending the presentations of students she works with. "It's hugely valuable," she says, "because I get to see students in 3D. I see what they are excited about, and I learn things about them that I wouldn't be privy to otherwise."

Students should also give their counselors a written description of their independent study projects, which the counselors refer to when writing a letter of recommendation. Students can also submit a project description via the "supplemental" portion of their application. Here is one example:

My independent study focuses on children in crisis. First I will study child refugees fleeing war-torn countries by reading accounts written by refugees and, if possible, by working with the International Rescue Committee. I'll also read books on how children deal with trauma and how their memories are affected by traumatic events. Sources include Mary Pipher's *The Middle of Everywhere: Helping Refugees Enter the American Community* and *God Grew Tired of Us* by John Bul Dau and Michael Sweeney.

Next I will focus on child soldiers. The reading for this trimester will be based primarily on outside assessments of this growing crisis, such as *Child Soldiers in Africa* by Alcinda Honwana and *Children at War* by P. W. Singer.

My last topic will be gender-based violence—what this term means, the implications of its use, and any possible legal remedies for this crime. My reading will include *Overcoming Violence Against Women and Girls* by Michael L. Penn and Rahel Nardos and *Gender Violence* by Astrid Aafjes and Anne Tierney Goldstein.

I meet with my mentor once a week and the director of independent study every other week to discuss what I have been reading and to prepare for the class I will teach once a trimester to the seminar, which meets five times in a ten-day cycle. At the end of each trimester I will write a paper, eight to ten pages long, based on my research.

I was initially interested in doing an independent study on these issues because I want to learn more about some of the heart-wrenching problems that afflict children around the world, from which we are often shielded. Having volunteered at the International Rescue Committee during the summer and having worked with children who endured hardships similar to those I will be reading about, my interest in this research grew.

Notice that this student describes the format—mentors, seminar meeting, presentations, and so forth. If the school's curriculum statement contains this information, there is no need to repeat it. (Be kind to those bleary, admissions-officers' eyes!)

Essays and interview

One more venue: if the project is particularly meaningful to the student, as many are, it may be an excellent essay topic that fits a few college Common Application prompts, including these:

- Discuss an accomplishment, event, or realization that sparked a period of personal growth and a new understanding of yourself or others.

- Describe a topic, idea, or concept you find so engaging that it makes you lose all track of time. Why does it captivate you? What or who do you turn to when you want to learn more?
- Share an essay on any topic of your choice. It can be one you've already written, one that responds to a different prompt, or one of your own design.

Remind students that an essay about independent study, if they choose to write one, should be more personal than a project description. They can focus on motivation for the project, what they hoped to accomplish, or how they met challenges along the way.

Another way independent study enters the post-high-school application process is through an interview. Not every college requires one, but many offer the opportunity to talk with a representative of the institution, often an alumnus. Other institutions of learning, as well as employers, also interview applicants. Many students have told me that they spoke at length about their independent study projects with interviewers. I am not surprised, given that the work they do in the course reveals much about their interests and priorities.

The Bottom Line

Does independent study enhance a student's profile in the application process? The answer is a definite maybe. An independent study project that arises from a passion for learning about the subject, one that shows a student's commitment, is a plus in all situations. A project that has neither of those qualities is neutral or may raise questions about why the student opted out of a more conventional class. Kaitlin Howrigan notes that applicants often state what they would like to study in college but "it really shows commitment if a student has explored a topic for a whole year." Her colleague Alex Bates agrees. Reflecting on his experience as a college admissions officer, Bates says, "When you see a self-directed student with an idea they are excited about, it reflects really positively." But he cautions that there is "no universal benefit of an independent study program. The school must be thoughtful about having students in the program who are really interested."

EMPLOYMENT MATTERS

The title of this section has a double meaning: *matters* as a noun meaning "practical concerns" and as a verb meaning "has significance." Both apply to teaching in an independent study program. The course exists within a school, which has a fixed budget and an array of course offerings.

Money first: the school has to figure out how to pay for an independent study program while being fair to all—seminar leaders, mentors, and anyone whose program draws funds from the school budget. Materials and equipment do not add up to much, but faculty salaries do. If independent study is a unit within a traditional course, you are home free (pun intended). If it is a stand-alone, there are a number of options:

- *replacement for one or two traditional courses in the teacher's schedule* I dropped two of my English classes to lead one seminar, mentor a sizable group of students, supervise students working with other mentors, recruit mentors and students, and order supplies. Independent study seminar replaced one other course in the schedule of a teacher who had no other supervisory duties.
- *stipend for extra duty* In some schools, independent study is an add-on to the usual schedule, compensated as an extracurricular activity. Budget constraints may make this option attractive, but to me, an arrangement like this seems not to acknowledge that independent study is a real class, one that consumes a substantial amount of teacher time.
- *full-time, faculty position* In this configuration independent study is essentially a separate department, with as many faculty as needed. This is the most expensive option, but in a school oriented to independent learning, it makes sense.

In all these scenarios, mentors are generally unpaid volunteers, though in some schools they receive a small honorarium. I am not aware of objections to independent study from teachers' unions, but if you are establishing a program in your school, it is a good idea to check what parameters, if any, govern mentorships. I have encountered concerns from teachers of other elective courses—legitimate concerns! A student's schedule is a pie: remove a slice for independent study, and there is one less portion for other classes. This gives rise to worries that an undersubscribed elective, and perhaps a job, will disappear. There is no easy solution. My belief is that the students' needs come first. Independent study is a pedagogical approach. If the principles underlying it are present in an elective, fine. If there is no existing path for students to pursue meaningful projects, the school should create one. I also believe that teachers are hardworking professionals and deserve respect. Thus no independent study project should duplicate an existing course, and no one should ever be pressured into a mentoring role.

BEYOND THE CLASSROOM YEARS

Teachers work in two time frames: the student sitting in the room now and the person that student will become someday. It is not unusual, I have found, for an independent study topic to relate to a future career. Jordan, who wrote a play for his independent study project, went on to become a Broadway producer; Josh tried (and failed) to start a school television station, but he is now a broadcast journalist. Karen, who wrote short stories for independent study, is a writing coach, with side gigs as a songwriter and performer. In her project on comedy writing, Val wrote skits about quirky historical events. She now turns her satiric eye on current news, and has a dual career as a screenwriter and stand-up comedian. Many students who did STEM projects now work for tech firms; a number have created and marketed popular apps, a few of which they created as part of their independent study projects. Of his independent study on carbon nanotubes, Will says, "That project set my life in motion on the track it is now, the core of who I am today," which is a scientist and engineer.

Skills strengthened by independent study can also lead to a career. Ed says that presentations were "great practice for future teachers" and adds, "if you can explain what you're doing, if you talk about it and show that you care about it, people respond positively." Ed responded so positively to his experience in independent study that he became a teacher himself. So did Kirsten. She marvels, "You're speaking, and a new idea is coming into someone's head that wasn't there before," a feeling she first experienced in seminar.

Even when there is no direct line to a future endeavor, the gifts of independent study remain. One of Gresa's takeaways came from one-on-one meetings with her mentor. "You have to succinctly put together an explanation of what you have done and what you will do next," she says. "That skill set is transferable. I use it now in conferences with my manager." She adds that independent study was an early experience in "leading something and talking about it, and I was able to build on that comfort in other situations." Jordyn polished his communication skills through his project on what was, at the time, the cutting edge of photography. He succeeded in explaining the complexities of digital cameras to the seminar. Now a cybersecurity adviser, he frequently meets with clients "who don't speak cyber-language" and must talk with them about technology solutions and cyber-risk in a way that is "interesting and relates to their individual business objectives."

Jordyn's project, like many, was an early stage of a lifelong interest. He continues to pursue photography and carefully records his travels, "taking the time to capture the image and frame it without editing people out in post-processing." One of his photos introduces this chapter. Kevin still makes time for poetry in the midst of a busy career and family life, just as he did when he juggled a full load of classes and activities in high school. He credits independent study for helping him understand an approach that suits him: "There was guidance, but independent study gave me space to work on my own. That's the way I like to work today." Jenny collaborated with students in other schools as part of her independent study, cold-calling until she found a group willing to work with her. "I reached out and gained enough self-confidence to talk to people I did not know," she says. "Those were muscles I hadn't gotten to flex before." She continued flexing those muscles in college and business school, where she cofounded a successful company. She now devotes time each week to advise young entrepreneurs, preparing the next generation to follow their own passions.

Sometimes independent study clarifies what the student does *not* want for the future. Zoe studied synesthesia, a condition in which sensory information picked up through one sense is processed by another (visual perception may be perceived as sound, scent as tactile, and so forth). Zoe herself is a synesthete. Her original plan was to study neurobiology after high school. Through her independent study, though, Zoe discovered she preferred big-picture narratives over technical scientific literature. She refocused her project on people's stories of living with synesthesia. After high school she went on to study architecture. Zoe doesn't regret her project: "I had to find out what I had to find out. It was nice to get a look at a subject, to peek at a field before college. Independent study lets you see for yourself what you like to do."

I'll borrow the last bit of Zoe's comment and turn it into a suggestion. Consider the independent study designs described in this book, and then "see for yourself what you like to do." Whether you implement a new program, tweak an existing program, or add a few independent study methods to your teacher's toolkit, your students will benefit. So will you, I firmly believe. Nurturing your students' intellectual and creative powers is immensely rewarding, and learning along with your students is quite a lot of fun! I wrote this book to move beyond my own classroom and share that joy.

Using Common Core Standards to Evaluate Projects

What do children need to learn, and when should they learn it? That question is hard enough to answer in a group as large as, say, two people. Imagine representatives from nearly all states, plus three territories and the District of Columbia, agreeing on a response. Yet that is what happened over the course of several years, when Common Core Standards were created, reviewed, and ultimately adopted in most of the United States. (Not without controversy, which continues to this day.) The standards pertain to math and language arts, with add-ons for social studies, science, and tech. They identify skills and concepts students should master each year from kindergarten through twelfth grade. The goal is to send well-prepared graduates off to the next step in their lives, whether it be additional schooling or employment.

Independent study is a method of learning, not a subject or a grade level. But because they provide a shared language for describing a project's educational content, Common Core Standards can be useful in evaluating a proposal or explaining its value to others—administrators, parents, and admissions or hiring officials, for example. To illustrate what I mean, here are a few examples of standards for grades eleven and twelve. The first pair are from the English language arts and literacy section, one for reading and one for writing, in that order:

- Cite strong and thorough textual evidence to support analysis of what the text says explicitly as well as inferences drawn from the text, including determining where the text leaves matters uncertain.
- Develop the topic thoroughly by selecting the most significant and relevant facts, extended definitions, concrete details, quotations, or other information and examples appropriate to the audience's knowledge of the topic.

These two come from the section devoted to history and social studies. Both address reading skills:

- Determine the central ideas or information of a primary or secondary source; provide an accurate summary that makes clear the relationships among the key details and ideas.
- Evaluate various explanations for actions or events and determine which explanation best accords with textual evidence, acknowledging where the text leaves matters uncertain.

Now, two standards for the reading of science and technical subjects:

- Compare and contrast findings presented in a text to those from other sources (including their own experiments), noting when the findings support or contradict previous explanations or accounts.
- Evaluate the hypotheses, data, analysis, and conclusions in a science or technical text, verifying the data when possible and corroborating or challenging conclusions with other sources of information.

This one addresses writing about social studies, science, or technical material:

- Develop claim(s) and counterclaims fairly and thoroughly, supplying the most relevant data and evidence for each while pointing out the strengths and limitations of both claim(s) and counterclaims in a discipline-appropriate form that anticipates the audience's knowledge level, concerns, values, and possible biases.

These examples express qualities you always look for when you are assessing your students' research notes and papers, I imagine, though perhaps you do not always articulate your criteria. Common Core Standards do this chore for you. You can access the whole set at www.corestandards .org. Don't be put off by the bureaucratic labels, which I have omitted here. Beneath the jargon lie sensible statements about learning.

Sample Forms

SAMPLE PROPOSAL FORM

Name: _____ Email: _____

Grade: _____ Phone: _____

Homeroom teacher: _____

Write a paragraph describing what you want to study and why. Include anything you want us to know as we evaluate your proposal.

_____

_____

_____

What question do you hope to answer over the course of a year working on your independent study?

_____

_____

_____

Do you have any idea what books, films, equipment, etc., you will need? If so, list them here.

_____

_____

_____

What challenges do you think you might face working independently?

_____

_____

_____

We will arrange for mentors, but you may suggest someone. No guarantees! Also, please do not approach the faculty member yourself.

SAMPLE WORK GRID: PROJECT ON OSCAR WILDE (WRITING, LIFE, AND TIMES)

Week of	Met with mentor? If no, explain.	What you discussed with mentor	Work you will do next week	Expectations met from the week before?
9/8	yes	summer reading: *The Picture of Dorian Gray* (Wilde)	read three articles in Norton Critical Edition	n/a
9/22	yes	discussed censorship of the original version (1890)	read Wilde's letters defending the book	yes
9/29	yes	analyzed Wilde's philosophy of art	compare published versions (1890 and 1891)	yes

Note: *Student's weekly notes should accompany this grid, along with source citations. The notes can be handwritten or typed, or students can attach photos of annotations in a text or of science and art work in progress.*

SAMPLE PRESENTATION PREP FORM

Name _____

Date of Presentation _____

Location _____

our classroom _____

online _____

hybrid _____

other location (specify) _____

If other, have you checked that the space is available and reserved it for our class? _____

Materials

What do you need? Be specific.

How many? One for each student, or can students share?

Are you supplying materials or do you want the school to provide them? (Note: the school may not have everything you are hoping to use. Ask! If need be, I will help you adjust your plan.)

Do you plan to distribute photocopies for homework or classwork? (Go green if you can, please.)

Homework _____ Classwork _____

Note: If the photocopies are for classwork, submit the original at least a week before the presentation. If you want to distribute the copies as a homework assignment, count back one week before you want to hand them out. Note: allow your classmates a week to complete your homework. If you are collecting their homework before your presentation, allow even more time and explain how they can submit their work to you. (I check all homework, so do not forget to give me copies or allow me access to their completed assignments.)

Technology

What do you need?

Do you know how to use it, or do you need a tutorial? If yes, ask me about when this might take place, and with whom.

If you are using video clips or interactive websites, check that they work and are accessible from the school computer system. (Be sure to keep track of your sources so you can cite them properly.)

Timeline

Work backward from your presentation date to fill in the dates when you must accomplish each task.

THREE WEEKS BEFORE _____
Discuss ideas with your mentor and with me. Think about both content and format.

TWO WEEKS BEFORE _____
Bring your detailed lesson plan to me. If you are using presentation slides, have them ready to show to me. If you are not already scheduled for a meeting, sign up on my calendar for an extra appointment.

ONE WEEK BEFORE _____
Invite your mentor to the presentation. Be polite, and do not be offended if the mentor can't attend. Sometimes the timing just does not work, but I will make sure that your mentor knows what/how you did.

Invite other teachers and friends, if you wish. Please let me know how many you expect to attend, so I can be sure there is enough room for all. If your presentation is virtual, give me the email addresses of your guests so I can send them the link.

Assign homework to your classmates (if you are giving homework). You can post the assignment on our class website or email it, or you can distribute paper copies.

WEEK OF _____
Email the final presentation script and your lesson plan to your mentor and to me.

Recheck the tech.

Remind your classmates via email what homework they should do and how/when they should turn it in.

SAMPLE STUDENT
SELF-ASSESSMENT FORM

Sources

List the sources you consulted. Include books, articles, films, podcasts, websites, interviews, musical recordings, and any other source of information. Were there any sources you wanted to consult but could not access? In the final product, are there any topics that lack sufficient sources? Which ones?

_____

_____

Content

What are three key points relating to your topic? Why are they important?

_____

_____

Who were the most important people involved in the events you researched? Why were they important?

_____

_____

How do the events you researched relate to current issues? Include both similarities and differences.

_____

_____

Time Management

List the dates for your interim goals as well as the dates you actually completed that stage of the work. If you missed a deadline, briefly explain why. Overall, how would you rate your time management for this project?

_____

_____

Writing

Briefly describe your writing process. How many drafts? What changed from the first to the final draft? What did you learn about your writing process as you worked on this project?

_____

_____

Overall Assessment

What is the most important thing you learned as you worked on this project? What else would you like to know?

_____

_____

Index

Academic Research Program (ARP), 63–65
adaptation(s)
    independent study–related, 59–75. *see also* independent study adaptations
administrators
    as mentors, 40
admissions officers
    independent study impact on, 127–30
advanced study
    foreign language independent study–related, 83
alumni
    as mentors, 40
annotation
    reading projects–related, 79
ARP. *see* Academic Research Program (ARP)
arts independent study, 92–95
    appreciation, history, 94–95
    performance and studio projects, 92–93
attendance record
    as factor in independent study, 34
    in homeschooling, 101–102
authorities. *see also* administrators
    homeschool independent study reporting to, 105–8

biology
    independent study units in, 118–19
boundary(ies)
    parent–child, 126

business professionals
    as mentors, 40

"Celebration of Research," 63, 124
classroom(s)
    independent study beyond, 123–34. *see also* independent study beyond classroom
college admissions
    course description, 127–28
    essays, 129–30
    independent study and, 127–30
    interview, 129–30
    project description, 128–29
Common Core Standards, 29
    in assessing independent study projects, 135–37
community-based independent study programs, 67–69
community resources
    as mentors, 40
confidence
    independent study–related, 4
content
    in independent study project proposal, 29
content specialists
    in independent study units within traditional class, 115
continuity
    power of, 18–21
    seminar format in harnessing, 19

course description
    college admissions–related, 127–28
    relevance to employment, 132–134
critical reading
    reading projects–related, 79
culture
    foreign language independent study–
        related, 83–84

disciplinary issues
    as factor in independent study, 35
disorganization
    as factor in independent study, 34

employment
    independent study impact on, 131–32
ending points
    of independent study projects, 13–14
engineering and technology
    independent study related to, 86–88.
    see also under technology and engineering
Engineering Event, 66–67
essay(s)
    college admissions–related, 129–30
expert(s)
    independent study project proposal–
        related consultations with, 28–32
    in independent study units within
        traditional class, 114

faculty
    as mentors, 39–40
feasibility
    of independent study project proposal,
        30
feedback
    independent study seminar–related,
        52–54
fieldwork projects
    science-related, 85–86
flexibility
    in independent study program, 6
    in independent study project proposal, 30
foreign language independent study,
    82–85
    advanced study, 83
    culture and, 83–84

language acquisition, 83
    linguistics in, 83
    presentation, 84
    translation in, 83
    writing in, 84

"gifted" students
    independent study not limited to, 3–4
goal(s)
    flexibility in, 30
    reaching for, 2
grade requirement(s)
    independent study program–related,
        11, 35

high school biology
    independent study units in, 118–19
homeschool independent study, 99–108
    curriculum description, 107–8
    mentoring for, 100–3, 108
    portfolio for, 106–7
    product, 108
    project, 100–3, 108
    reporting to authorities, 105–8
    seminar, 103–5, 108
    transcript for, 106–7
hybrid independent study format, 72–75

independent study. *see also specific types*
    and subject areas, e.g., language arts
    independent study
    adaptations, 59–75. *see also* indepen-
        dent study adaptations
    advantages of, 1–2
    arts-related, 92–95. *see also* arts inde-
        pendent study
    attendance record as factor in, 34
    benefits of, 12–13
    beyond classroom, 123–34. *see also*
        independent study beyond classroom
    in breaking barriers, 13–14
    college admissions related to, 127–30
    confidence gained through, 4
    in current times, 2–3
    described, 4–5
    disciplinary issues related to, 35
    elements of, 99

employment impact of, 131–32
foreign language, 82–85. *see also under* foreign language independent study
not limited to "gifted" students, 3–4
grade requirements for, 11, 35
homeschool, 99–108. *see also* homeschool independent study
interdisciplinary, 95–97
language arts, 78–82. *see also* language arts independent study
learning issues related to, 34–35
as legitimate course, 124–25
mathematics, 89–90
middle school, 65–67, 119–20
motivation in, 11
noncredit, 69–72
parent–child boundaries, 126
problems impacting, 34–37
programs, 9–25. *see also under* independent study program(s)
projects, 12–17, 27–46. *see also specific types and* independent study project(s)
reasons for, 2–3
sample forms, 139–44. *see also specific types and* sample forms
social studies projects, 90–92. *see also* social studies independent study
STEM projects, 85–90. *see also under specific subject areas and* STEM independent study
students in, 3–4
subject area courses and, 116–18
subject area tips, 77–97. *see also under specific subject and* subject area tips
time management issues, 35
topics for, 61–62
within traditional class, 109–21. *see also* independent study units within traditional class
independent study adaptations, 59–75
community-based programs, 67–69
hybrid formats, 72–75
long-form program, 63–65
middle school independent study, 65–67

noncredit programs, 69–72
one class, one teacher, 60–63
school-based, 59–75
topics, 61–62
virtual formats, 72–75
independent study beyond classroom, 123–34
case examples, 132–34
college admissions related to, 127–30. *see also under* college admissions
employment-related, 131–32
initiatives related to, 124–25
parent–child boundaries, 126
independent study presentation(s), 3, 47–58, 79–94. *see also* independent study seminar
independent study program(s), 9–25. *see also under* independent study
adult guidance in, 5–6
basics of, 10–12
community-based, 67–69
elements of, 5–6
flexibility in, 6
grade requirement for entry, 11
long-form, 63–65
performance in, 6
student power and responsibility in, 5
types of, 11, 12
independent study project(s), 12–17, 27–46
assessing, 44–46
case study, 13–17
Common Core Standards in assessing, 29, 135–37
ending points of, 13–14
homeschool-related, 100–3, 108
matching student with, 34–37
mathematics-related, 89
mentors' role in, 37–44. *see also under* mentor(s)
problems impacting, 34–37
social studies–related, 90
starting point for, 14–15
students say-so in designing, 28
technology and engineering–related, 87
types of, 11, 12

independent study project proposal
consulting experts for help in evaluating, 28–32
content in, 29
conversation about, 28–32
evaluation factors, 28–32
feasibility of, 30
first-draft problems, 32–33
flexibility in, 30
originality of, 29
readiness for, 32–33
sample forms, 139–44. *see also specific
types and* sample forms
skill development in, 29
solidity of, 30
sustainability of, 29–30
independent study seminar, 3, 11, 17–21,
47–58, 127–28. *see also under*
seminar(s)
feedback, 52–54
grading, 54–55
managing a discussion, 48–49
preparing students for presentations,
48–52
scheduling, 55–58
teaching tips, 50–52
independent study units within traditional class, 109–21
adult guidance, 113–14
assessing, 114
content specialists in, 115
high school biology, 118–19
inviting visitors, 114
mentors in, 114
middle school science, 119–20
photography, 120–21
student leadership, 110–12
students teaching peers in, 114–16
subject-area courses and, 116–18
interdisciplinary independent study,
95–97
"interdisciplinary independent study
seminar," 2–3
interview
college admissions–related, 129–30

lab projects
science-related, 86

language(s)
foreign, 82–85. *see also under* foreign
language independent study
language acquisition
foreign language independent study–
related, 83
language arts independent study, 78–82
reading projects, 78–81. *see also under*
reading projects
writing projects, 81–82. *see also under*
writing projects
leadership
student, 110–12. *see also under* student
leadership
learning
independent study emphasis on,
13–14
learning issues
independent study–related, 34–35
linguistics
foreign language independent study–
related, 83
long-form independent study program,
63–65

mathematics
independent study related to, 89–90
presentation, 89–90
product, 89
projects, 89
mentor(s)
administrators as, 40
alumni as, 40
business professionals as, 40
community resources as, 40
faculty as, 39–40
finding, 39–42
homeschool independent study–
related, 100–3, 108
role of, 37–44
staff as, 40
supporting, 42–44
types of, 39–42
mentor–student relationship, 37–44. *see
also under* mentor(s)
middle school independent study, 65–67
middle school science
independent study units in, 119–20

"mini independent study," 117–18
motivation
    in independent study, 11, 14–15

news coverage comparison seminar,
    21–23, 23*t*
noncredit independent study, 69–72

opt-out assignment
    in independent study units within
    traditional class, 112
originality
    of independent study project proposal, 29

parent–child boundaries
    independent study beyond classroom–
    related, 126
performance
    in independent study program, 6
    writing projects–related, 82
performance and studio projects
    arts-related, 92–93
photography
    independent study units in, 120–21
poor grades
    as factor in independent study, 35
poor skills
    as factor in independent study, 35
portfolio
    homeschool independent study–
    related, 106–7
preparing students for presentations
    independent study seminar–related,
    48–52
presentation(s)
    foreign language independent study–
    related, 84
    independent study, 3, 11, 47–58,
    79–84. *see also* independent study
    seminar
    mathematics-related, 89–90
    multiple, 20–21
    reading projects–related, 79–80
    science-related, 86
    social studies–related, 91
    technology and engineering–related,
    87
    writing projects–related, 82

problem(s)
    budget, 3–5, 30
    independent study project–related,
    34–37
    legitimacy, 124–125
    space, 10–12, 30, 85–90, 92–95
    staffing, 3–5, 37–44, 102, 114,
    131–132
product(s)
    homeschool independent study–
    related, 108
    as independent study project ending
    point, 13–14
    independent study–related, 3
    mathematics-related, 89
    reading projects–related, 79
    social studies–related, 90–91
professional associations
    as source for mentors, 40
project(s)
    homeschool independent study–
    related, 100–3, 108
    independent study–related, 12–17,
    27–46. *see also* independent study
    project(s)
proposal(s)
    first-draft problems, 32–33
    independent study project–related,
    28–33. *see also* independent study
    project proposal
publication
    writing projects–related, 82

reading
    critical, 79
    in writing projects, 81
reading projects, 78–81
    annotation, 79
    critical reading, 79
    in language arts independent study,
    78–81
    mentor reading, 78–79, 81
    presentation, 79–80
    product, 79
    student workload, 78
relationship(s)
    mentor–student, 37–44. *see also under*
    mentor(s)

resource(s)
  borrowed or shared, 30, 85–90
  budget, 3–5, 30
  community, 40
  legitimacy, 124–125
  space, 10–12, 30, 85–90, 92–95
  staffing, 3–5, 37–44, 102, 114,
    131–132
  reference material (library), 30, 78–82,
    85-90, 90–92
responsibility(ies)
  students', 5

sample forms, 139–44
  independent study–related, 139–44
  sample presentation prep form,
    141–42
  sample proposal form, 139–40
  sample student self-assessment form,
    143–44
  sample work grid, 140
sample presentation prep form, 141–42
sample proposal form, 139–40
sample student self-assessment form,
  143–44
sample work grid, 140
"scaffolding curriculum," 63
scheduling
  independent study seminar–related,
    55–58
"Scholars Symposium," 124
school-based independent study
  options for, 59–75. *see also* indepen-
    dent study adaptations
science, 85–86
  fieldwork projects, 85–86
  independent study related to,
    85–86
  lab projects, 86
  middle school, 119–20
  presentations, 86
  research from written sources, 86
seminar(s)
  described, 21
  harnessing continuity, 19
  homeschool independent study–
    related, 103–5, 108

independent study, 3, 11, 17–21,
  47–58, 127–28. *see also* indepen-
    dent study seminar
  interdependence of, 19–20
  multiple opportunities to present in,
    20–21
  presentation examples, 21–25, 23*t*
  student as teacher in, 17–21
skill development
  in independent study project proposal,
    29
skill specialists
  in independent study units within
    traditional class, 115
skills-related issues
  as factor in independent study, 35
social studies independent study, 90–92
  presentation, 91
  products, 90–91
  projects, 90
specialist(s)
  in independent study units within
    traditional class, 115
staff
  as mentors, 40
starting point(s)
  for independent study project, 14–15
STEM independent study, 85–90. *see
    also under specific subject areas, e.g.,*
    mathematics
  educational value of, 85
  mathematics, 89–90
  science, 85–86
  technology and engineering, 86–87
student(s)
  designing independent study project
    by, 28
  "gifted," 3–4
  in independent study, 3–4
  leadership by, 110–12. *see also under*
    student leadership
  matching independent study project
    with, 34–37
  power of, 5
  responsibility of, 5
  seminar in strengthening interdepen-
    dence of, 19–20

as teacher, 17–21
teaching peers, 114–16
student leadership
in independent study units within
traditional class, 110–12
opt-out assignment, 112
student–mentor relationship, 37–44. *see
also under* mentor(s)
students teaching peers
in independent study units within
traditional class, 114–16
student workload
reading projects–related, 78
subject area courses
in independent study units within
traditional class, 116–18
subject area tips, 77–97. *see also under
specific subject, e.g.,* language arts
independent study
arts, 92–95. *see also* arts independent
study
foreign language, 82–85. *see also* foreign language independent study
interdisciplinary, 95–97
language arts, 78–82. *see also* language
arts independent study
social studies, 90–92. *see also* social
studies independent study
STEM, 85–90. *see also specific subject
areas and* STEM independent study
"symposium," 124

teacher(s)
student as, 17–21

technology and engineering, 86–87
independent study related to, 86–87
presentations, 87
projects, 87
time management issues
independent study–related, 35
topic(s)
for independent study, 61–62
traditional class
independent study units within,
109–21. *see also* independent study
units within traditional class
transcript(s)
described, 106–7
homeschool independent study–
related, 106–7
translation
foreign language independent study–
related, 83

virtual independent study format,
72–75

writing projects, 81–84
foreign language independent study–
related, 84
language arts independent study–
related, 81–82
mentor's role in, 81
workload, 81–82
performance, 82
presentation, 82
publication, 82
reading in, 81

About the Author

GERALDINE WOODS established the independent study program at the Horace Mann School and directed it for twenty-five years. She has also taught every level of English, from fifth grade through AP, and currently teaches adult writing classes. An award-winning teacher, she created dozens of curricular units on writing and close reading and shared her independent study design with schools throughout the United States and in Europe, Asia, and Australia. Woods is the author of more than 50 books; her most recent are *25 Great Sentences and How They Got That Way* (Norton, 2020) and *Sentence. A Period-to-Period Guide to Building Better Readers and Writers* (Norton, 2021). She posts wry commentary on language on her blog, grammarianinthecity.com.